J. Q. ADAMS

ENCYCLOPEDIA
of PRESIDENTS

John Quincy Adams

Sixth President of the United States

By Zachary Kent

Consultant: Charles Abele, Ph.D.
Social Studies Instructor
Chicago Public School System

 CHILDRENS PRESS ®
CHICAGO

A peace medal commemorating a treaty between the United States
and an Indian tribe during John Quincy Adams's presidency

Library of Congress Cataloging-in-Publication Data

Kent, Zachary.
   John Quincy Adams.

   (Encyclopedia of presidents)
   Includes index.
   Summary: A biography of the sixth president, who
continued the family dedication to public service begun
by his father, the second president of the United
States.
   1.   Adams, John Quincy, 1767-1848—Juvenile literature.
2.   Presidents—United States—Biography—Juvenile
literature.   [1.   Adams, John Quincy, 1767-1848.
2.   Presidents]   I.   Title.   II.   Series.
E377.K38.   1987   973.5'5'0924 [B] [92]   86-31022
ISBN 0-516-01386-6

Childrens Press, Chicago
Copyright ©1987 by Regensteiner Publishing Enterprises, Inc.
All rights reserved. Published simultaneously in Canada.
Printed in the United States of America.
   7 8 9 10 R 96 95

Picture Acknowledgments

The Bettmann Archive—5, 10 (top), 25 (right),
29, 38, 43, 48, 49, 52, 57, 58 (right), 59, 60, 66,
74 (top), 76, 81, 84, 85, 88, 89
H. Armstrong Roberts—12 (left), 13, 16, 32, 35,
36, 37, 39, 42 (left), 58 (left), 82
Historical Pictures Service—6, 27, 40 (top), 44,
45, 46 (bottom), 50 (top), 62, 67, 72, 74
(bottom), 75, 87
Library of Congress—10 (bottom), 25 (left), 55
Nawrocki Stock Photo—4 (2 photos), 78
North Wind Picture Archives—12 (right), 15,
17, 19, 20, 22, 28, 30, 40 (bottom), 42 (center
and right), 46 (top), 53, 70, 80
U.S. Bureau of Printing and Engraving—2, 50
(bottom), 71 (2 photos)
Cover design and illustration by
Stephen Gaston Dobson

The home of John Quincy Adams

Table of Contents

Chapter 1   Introduction 7
Chapter 2   Early Years Abroad 11
Chapter 3   Beginning a Life of Public Service 23
Chapter 4   Return to Russia 33
Chapter 5   Peacemaker and Diplomat 41
Chapter 6   Secretary of State 51
Chapter 7   President of the United States 61
Chapter 8   To Fall and Rise Again 77
Chapter 9   Old Man Eloquent 83
Chronology of American History 90
Index 99

Chapter 1

Introduction

A terrible uproar shook the room from the Speaker's chair to the balcony seats. Congressmen shouted angrily until they made themselves hoarse. Then they stamped their feet and banged their desks. Keeping up the deafening noise, they refused to let John Quincy Adams speak in the House of Representatives.

In 1836, Adams was the most hated congressman in the United States. The *New York Times* branded him "the Massachusetts Madman." Ugly letters arrived for him almost every day. A Georgia man warned, "You will be shot down in the street." An Alabama writer threatened, "I promise to cut your throat from ear to ear."

The old man from Quincy, Massachusetts, remained fearless. "The best actions of my life," he confided to his diary, "make me nothing but Enemies."

John Quincy Adams had already served as president of the United States from 1825 to 1829. But restless in retirement, he gladly returned to Washington in 1831 as a congressman. In the rising dispute over slavery, antislavery people, called abolitionists, sent Adams formal letters demanding an end to slavery. Dutifully, Adams presented these petitions to the House of Representatives. Most of the petitions concerned slave trade in the District of Columbia, where the nation's capital lay. But congressmen from all over the South feared that the slavery system was in danger. They decided to crush further debate on the issue. In 1836, by a vote of 117 to 68, the House passed a resolution stating that all slavery petitions should be laid aside without discussion.

Stung by this "gag rule," Congressman Adams immediately jumped to his feet. Though he was a small, bald man almost seventy years old, his shrill voice still could echo through the marble columns of the chamber.

"I hold the resolution to be a direct violation of the Constitution of the United States!"

His fellow congressmen howled him down, but Adams was not afraid of a fight. For the next eight years he struggled almost alone to regain the right to petition. Week after week Adams hounded the members of the House. His attacks were as "fierce as ten furies," remarked Representative Andrew Johnson. The Speaker of the House hammered his gavel every time the stubborn old man jumped to his feet with a comment about slavery. Savage screams of "Order! Order!" poured from a hundred congressmen as they tried to drown him out.

"I see where the shoe pinches, Mr. Speaker," coolly answered Adams after one such outburst. "It will pinch more yet. I'll deal out to the gentlemen a diet that they'll find . . . hard to digest."

Excited abolitionists kept sending him petitions. On an

especially busy day, for example, he presented 350 of them. The House put them all aside without examination. Adams eventually offered so many petitions that, seventy years later, a historian discovered the Capitol janitor still using the paper to light the fire in his basement stove!

As the bitter contest over petitioning continued, Adams's toughness slowly won him respect. His admirers began calling him "Old Man Eloquent" because of his intelligence and courage. Taking a tour through the North in 1843, Adams suddenly found himself a hero. In town after town, crowds greeted his train with torchlit parades and happy shouting. In Rochester, New York, cannon boomed and church bells rang upon his arrival.

Clearly the people demanded their right to petition. John Quincy Adams returned to Congress and battled until resistance caved in. In December 1844, he saw the gag rule overturned by a vote of 105 to 80. The debate over slavery could finally resume in the House of Representatives.

At the age of seventy-seven, Adams had scored perhaps his greatest triumph. Many other successes marked his fifty years of public service. Following in the tradition of his father, second U.S. president John Adams, John Quincy Adams strongly believed in the importance of duty and justice. In a long life that ranged from the American Revolution to the heart of the slavery struggle, he remained forever true to his high ideals. As a young man he mistakenly wrote, "I am good for nothing and cannot even carry myself forward in the world." How lucky that John Quincy Adams was not predicting his future value to his country.

Above: The birthplace of John Quincy Adams (left) and his father, John Adams (right)
Below: John Quincy Adams's room in his parents' house

Chapter 2

Early Years Abroad

John Quincy Adams was born on July 11, 1767, in Braintree (afterwards renamed Quincy), Massachusetts. His birthplace, a simple two-story wooden house with a long roof sloping down in the back, still stands today. Next door is the house where his father, John Adams, was born in 1735. As the first son of John Adams and his wife, Abigail Smith Adams, the boy was immersed in American history from his early childhood.

In the late 1760s, the Massachusetts colony was already rumbling with the talk of revolution. Many people throughout the American colonies hated the unfair taxes England thrust upon them. "No taxation without representation!" men shouted at town meetings. These angry colonists demanded a voice in the British parliament and insisted on being treated as well as other British citizens.

An ambitious, outspoken lawyer, John Quincy's father soon took up the cause of liberty. Though his political work often carried him far from home, John Adams still

John Quincy Adams's parents,
Abigail and John

showed a real interest in his children's education. To his wife he wrote, "Take care that they don't go astray. Cultivate their Minds, inspire their little Hearts. . . . Fix their Attention upon great and glorious Objects, sort out every little Thing, weed out every Meanness."

With his intelligent, strong-willed mother as a guide, little John Quincy began his studies. In his earliest letter, the modest six-year-old boy admitted he spent "too much of my time in play [th]ere is a great deal of room for me to grow better." The next year, instead of going to the town school, he was tutored by two of his father's law clerks. While John Adams attended the Continental Congress in Philadelphia, he received his first letter from his son. In it the boy revealed that he had "been trying ever since you went away to learn to write you a Letter. I shall make poor work of it, but . . . Mamma says . . . that my duty to you may be expressed in poor writings as well as good."

BOSTON

The British attack on Bunker Hill

Before young John Quincy reached the age of eight, the long-awaited Revolution broke out in Massachusetts. On April 19, 1775, regular British soldiers skirmished with defiant rebel militiamen. In the towns of Lexington and Concord, the noise of musket fire filled the air until dozens of brave colonists lay dead and wounded. Now England understood that Americans were determined to resist British rule, even if it meant bloodshed.

In June a sound like thunder rolled down the Massachusetts coast. Climbing with his mother to the summit of nearby Penn Hill, John Quincy saw billows of smoke rising from a battlefield several miles to the north. He glimpsed tongues of flame spouting from the cannons on Bunker Hill, near Boston. The fight for independence urged by John Quincy's father was going on just a few miles from home. Soon, citizens fearing the growing danger in Boston rushed to the safety of suburbs such as Braintree. For a time friends, relatives, and strangers crowded into the Adams house.

13

In the spring of 1776 General George Washington's continental army forced the British soldiers to abandon Boston. With the return of peace to Massachusetts, John Quincy continued his education. The boy always loved books and could often be found reading *The Arabian Nights* or perhaps a play by Shakespeare. Of his studies he wrote to his father, "I make but a poor figure at composition, my head is much too fickle, my thoughts are running after birds' eggs, play and trifles till I get vexed with myself."

At the age of ten an event occurred that drastically changed John Quincy's life. The Continental Congress in Philadelphia sent John Adams on an important diplomatic mission in France. "By earnest entreaty" John Quincy persuaded his father to take him along. On February 13, 1778, the two Adamses boarded the twenty-four gun frigate *Boston*, commanded by Captain Samuel Tucker. The ship's six-week voyage across the Atlantic proved exciting and dangerous. A British warship chased them for a while. Then during a hurricane lightning struck the *Boston*, killing four of its sailors. Later the *Boston* captured a British merchant ship and took possession of its cargo. Finally, at the end of March, they reached the coast of France.

Except for a short visit home in 1779, John Quincy Adams would spend his next seven years in Europe. Before taking up his diplomatic chores in Paris, John Adams found a school for his son. At the Passy Academy John Quincy studied hard. In surprise his father remarked, "This child . . . learned more French in a day than I could learn in a Week with all my books."

The Dutch city of Leiden, where John Quincy Adams attended school

A visit to the Dutch city of Leiden persuaded John Adams that his son should study there. For two years the boy attended Leiden University, where he learned Latin, Greek, and other subjects. He also took time to have fun, ice-skating on the frozen Dutch canals in the winter and riding horseback past country windmills during warmer weather.

By the time of his fourteenth birthday, John Quincy had grown into a handsome, sophisticated young man. Hearing that American diplomat Francis Dana was searching for a secretary and interpreter to travel with him to Russia, John Quincy Adams volunteered. With his father's consent, he set off with Dana on this new adventure. For two months they journeyed across Eastern Europe until they arrived in Saint Petersburg, the Russian capital.

This statue of Peter the Great was erected in Saint Petersburg in 1782, the same year John Quincy Adams lived there.

With great surprise, the boy noticed differences between the peasants and the nobility in Saint Petersburg. "There is nobody here but Slaves and Princes," he soon wrote to his mother. Without any companions his own age and with few American comrades, John Quincy Adams worked and studied in Russia for a year. From Massachusetts his older sister, Abigail, wrote him a loving letter. "You, my Brother, are far, very far removed from your friends and connections, it is a painful reflection to those who have parted with a Son and Brother."

After more than a year in Saint Petersburg, Francis Dana was never received by the Russian government. Called back at last by his father, John Quincy departed the Russian capital on October 30, 1782. In the company of an Italian friend, Count Greco, the teenager traveled by sled and carriage over the frozen rivers and across the snow-

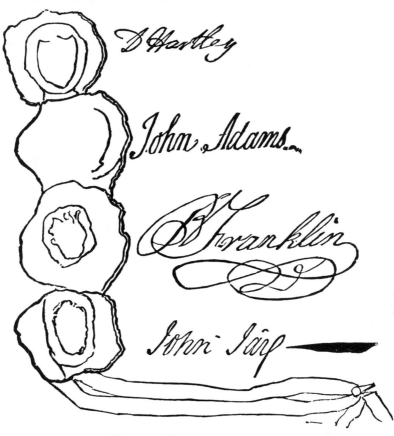

Signatures on the Treaty of Paris

covered countryside of Sweden, Denmark, and northern Germany. Through most of this winter trip the weather was terrible, but John Quincy enjoyed the friendly people and strange sights of these foreign lands.

Finally, on April 20, 1783, he rejoined his joyful father in The Hague, the capital city of Holland. John Adams was in Holland to arrange a large loan of money for the new United States government. He, Benjamin Franklin, and John Jay had negotiated a peace treaty with British commissioners in Paris. This Treaty of Paris, signed on September 3, 1783, marked the formal end of the American Revolution. After eight years of bloody struggle, the United States was free at last.

During the next two years, John Quincy Adams continued his studies in Holland and France. He also assisted his father as a private secretary. In Paris John Adams's diplomatic duties were to arrange trade treaties with England and other European nations. This was extremely important if the United States was to survive its earliest years.

A happy reunion for John Quincy occurred in the summer of 1784. His mother and sister were on their way to join him and his father in Paris. Unable to get away, John Adams sent John Quincy to meet them in London. To his wife he wrote he was sending "a Son who is the greatest Traveller of his age, and . . . as promising and manly a youth as in the whole world." When Abigail Adams finally saw her son again, she could recognize him only by his eyes, he had changed so much in six years.

John Quincy remained in France with his parents and sister until the following spring. Then he decided to finish his education in the United States. With a sense of patriotism for the country he had not seen since he was twelve, he exclaimed, "In America I can live *independent* and *free;* and rather than live otherwise I would wish to die."

Admitted to Harvard College as a junior, the eighteen-year-old began a two-year course of study. On visits to Braintree he impressed his country relatives with the size of his European wardrobe: sixty-five pairs of stockings, four pair of shoes, and many articles of clothing in his favorite colors of black and blue. Some of his cousins and classmates admired John Quincy's worldly manners and opinions. Others, however, decided he was too stiff and

John Quincy Adams attended Harvard College in Cambridge, Massachusetts

snobbish. Having grown up in the company of adults, John Quincy was often severe on himself and critical of others.

Following his Harvard graduation in July 1787, John Quincy Adams entered the law office of Theophilus Parsons in Newburyport, Massachusetts. There he worked as a clerk for three years while he learned the law. Worried about his future, he claimed he felt a certain "weakness of spirit." Still he labored up to twelve hours a day. He realized that in Newburyport "without friends or connections I am to stand on my own ground."

19

Adams probably strolled through Boston Common, a public park,
during his four years as a young lawyer in Boston.

August 1790 found twenty-three-year-old John Quincy
Adams walking the cobbled streets of Boston. His education finished, the young man rented an office on Court
Street and set himself up as a lawyer. His father, after
serving as minister to Great Britain, had become the first
vice-president of the United States in 1789.

When the radical author Thomas Paine attacked the
new federal government in a pamphlet called *The Rights
of Man*, John Quincy Adams defended President George
Washington's policies with a series of articles signed with
the name "Publicola." In one he chided, "Mr. Paine seems
to think it is as easy for a nation to change its government,
as for a man to change his coat." Many people admired
these writings and wondered who Publicola was. Some
believed the writer was John Adams. A few guessed it was
his son.

Thomas Paine, in his pamphlet *The Rights of Man,* defended the French Revolution and the rights of the common citizen. England considered him a traitor for his views, and he moved to France. But French radicals thought Paine's views were too conservative, and he was imprisoned there for a year. Paine resented George Washington for not having helped to get him out of prison.

RIGHTS OF MAN:

BEING AN

ANSWER TO MR. BURKE's ATTACK

ON THE

FRENCH REVOLUTION.

BY

THOMAS PAINE,

SECRETARY FOR FOREIGN AFFAIRS TO CONGRESS IN THE AMERICAN WAR, AND AUTHOR OF THE WORK INTITLED *COMMON SENSE.*

LONDON:
PRINTED FOR J. JOHNSON, ST PAUL's CHURCH-YARD.
MDCCXCI.

While waiting for law clients over the next two years, John Quincy Adams wrote other articles supporting the sometimes unpopular views of President Washington. All across the country, Americans scanned the newspapers and marveled at the wisdom of the mystery writer, who now signed himself "Marcellus" and "Columbus."

Adams's arguments proved so forceful that President Washington took notice of him. Impressed with the young lawyer, Washington appointed him United States minister to Holland in 1794. As a lawyer who had lived in Holland and knew the language, John Quincy Adams seemed a perfect choice for the position. Vice-President Adams beamed with pride at the advancement of his "good and worthy son," claiming, "All my hopes are in him, both for my family and country." Having decided to accept the "very unexpected" position, at the age of twenty-six John Quincy Adams set out on his long career in public service.

The Hague was Holland's capital from 1795 to 1808. John Quincy Adams served there as minister to Holland from 1794 to 1797.

Chapter 3

Beginning a Life
of Public Service

With his younger brother Thomas, hired as his secretary, John Quincy Adams sailed out of Boston on the ship *Alfred*. The leaky vessel caused the Adams brothers some nervousness. Later John Quincy commented, "I think hereafter I'll avoid embarking in an eggshell to cross the Atlantic."

In England John Quincy performed his first diplomatic duty. He delivered to American ambassador John Jay a trunk full of important diplomatic papers. Adams was relieved to hand over the papers. On the ride from the British seacoast to London the trunk broke loose from its carriage straps. Luckily, Adams heard a strange thump in the road and stopped the coach. Leaping to the ground, he found the trunk lying in the dust. The papers locked inside were essential to John Jay in treaty negotiations with the British.

When John Quincy arrived in Holland at last, he found the country gripped in war. An invading French army had thrown the little nation into turmoil. "The fate of the Netherlands is suspended," John Quincy exclaimed to his father. As America's official representative in Holland, the young ambassador did his best to protect United States citizens and their property. Soon thousands of French troops took up quarters in The Hague. "We are quiet and in danger of nothing but hunger," John Quincy wrote to calm his mother. Regularly the young minister sent reports on the European situation to the United States. Secretary of State Edmund Randolph called these impressive dispatches "well digested, well arranged and well connected."

While he waited for the formation of a new Dutch government, John Quincy returned to England. With free time on his hands, the young diplomat began calling at the elegant Tower Hill home of London's American consul. Joshua Johnson had seven lovely daughters, who made visiting a pleasure. In his unusual Dutch-style clothes, John Quincy attended the theatre, went to dances, and visited art galleries with the Johnsons. In the evenings he often dined with the family and later enjoyed listening to the Johnson sisters entertain with singing and music.

Twenty-two-year-old Louisa Catherine Johnson especially attracted his attention, though she later remembered, "I never observed anything in Mr. Adams . . . towards me that indicated the smallest preference." Though Adams considered himself a "sullen and silent" suitor, early in 1796 he openly proclaimed his love for her,

Left: Louisa Catherine Johnson, Adams's wife
Right: John Quincy Adams in 1795, at the age of 28

and soon they were engaged. For months at a time John Quincy's duties in Holland kept the couple apart, but finally on July 26, 1797, he and Louisa were married.

A month earlier, Adams had received a new commission from the United States. President Washington picked him to be minister to Portugal. "Consider the new appointment," advised the secretary of state, "a decided proof of the President's high opinion of your talent, integrity and worth."

But before the ambassador and his wife could leave for Portugal, an even more important dispatch arrived from America. After eight years, George Washington had retired from the office of president. And John Adams had been chosen to follow him as second president of the United States.

John Adams worried about what people would say if he kept a relative on the government payroll. George Washington, however, insisted: "Your son . . . is the most valuable public character we have abroad." He urged John Adams to keep his son in diplomatic service. Finally Adams agreed, exclaiming, "the sons of Presidents have the same claim to liberty, equality, and the benefit of the laws with all other citizens." In need of a skilled ambassador in Prussia, he named his son to that post.

In the fall of 1797, John Quincy Adams journeyed with his new wife to Berlin to take up his duties there. At the city gates their carriage was halted by a guard who almost refused the new ambassador entry into the capital city. Angrily Adams remembered being questioned "by a dapper lieutenant who did not know, until one of his private soldiers explained to him, who the United States were."

The newlyweds took an apartment on the Bearen Strasse. Though they employed a butler, two maids, a footman, a coachman, and a cook, the Adamses lived more modestly than most of the city's foreign diplomats. Louisa herself sewed the bed-curtains for the unheated bedroom she shared with her husband. For the next four years, Adams labored to strengthen relations between the United States and the Prussian government of King Frederick William. Though John Quincy seemed to have little faith in himself, his mission was a great success.

After a rocky, often unpopular term as president, John Adams, a member of the Federalist party, stepped down in 1801 as Democratic-Republican Thomas Jefferson became the third president of the United States. Happy to be free

Adams's farm in Quincy, Massachusetts

of ugly party politics, John Adams retired to his farm in Quincy. Soon John Quincy received a letter from his mother hinting, "We have been a scattered family. If some of my children could now be collected round the parent Hive . . . it would add much to the happiness of our declining years."

In the spring of 1801 John Quincy Adams, with his wife and infant son, sailed for the United States "to begin the world anew," as he put it. Louisa Adams, after growing up in European society as the daughter of a diplomat, found the simple life in Massachusetts very strange. "Had I stepp'd into Noah's ark," she admitted, "I do not think I could have been more utterly astonished."

For a year John Quincy resisted getting involved with politics. Like his father, he wished to be "a man of my whole country" rather than connected to a single political party. In February 1803, though, the Federalist-controlled Massachusetts legislature elected John Quincy Adams to a six-year term in the United States Senate.

A view of Washington, D.C., in 1800

Washington, D.C., was still a crude, unfinished city when the new senator arrived there. At one end of long Pennsylvania Avenue stood the President's Mansion. At the other end, on a rising hill, stood the impressive Capitol building. Between the two lay broad, empty fields and ramshackle houses. With every rain the wide road turned into a sea of mud. Shocked to think she would have to live in such a place, Louisa Adams called the city a "scene of utter desolation."

Taking his place in the Senate chamber, thirty-five-year-old Adams immediately angered his fellow Federalists. Against their wishes he supported President Jefferson's purchase of the vast Louisiana Territory. "Curse on

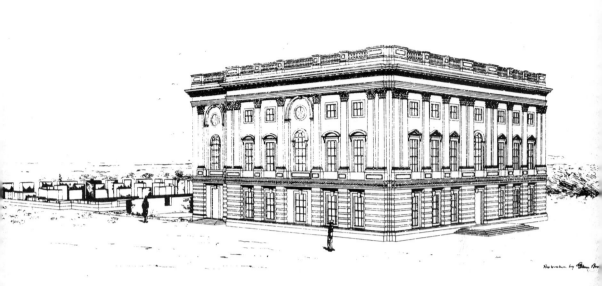

The Capitol Building in 1800, when Congress first occupied it

the stripling," swore Federalist Theodore Lyman, "how he apes the sire!" Soon Federalists realized that Adams, like his father, was an independent thinker.

"I do not disapprove of your conduct in the business of Louisiana," the elder Adams wrote to his son, "though I know it will become a very unpopular subject in the northern states. . . . I think you have been right!" In his diary John Quincy noted, "I have already had occasion to experience . . . the danger of adhering to my own principles." Rather than blindly obey the urgings of Federalist leaders, however, he determined to follow his conscience.

In the summer of 1807 Great Britain was locked in a war with France. On the Atlantic Ocean, English warships stopped American vessels, searched them, and forced or "impressed" sailors to serve in the British navy. The merchants and shipbuilders of New England greatly relied on trade with Europe. But when the British man-of-war

The British take four men from the *Chesapeake*. This event led to the Embargo Act of 1807 and helped set the stage for the War of 1812.

Leopard fired on the American naval frigate *Chesapeake*, killing several men, John Quincy Adams called for a quick response. He joined President Jefferson in demanding a British trade embargo that would cut off American business abroad.

When the embargo bill reached the Senate floor for consideration, Adams remarked to a friend, "This measure will cost you and me our seats. . . . But private interest must not be put in opposition to public good." With Senator Adams's help, the Embargo Act of 1807 passed.

As U.S. merchant fleets fell idle in New England's harbors, people became outraged. They blamed Adams for their troubles and regarded him a traitor. The Northhampton *Hampshire Gazette* called him, "A party scavenger! One of those ambitious politicians who lives on both land and water . . . but who finally settles down in the mud." The Salem *Gazette* condemned Adams as "a popularity seeker . . . courting the prevailing party." In September a meeting of Massachusetts Federalists angrily concluded that Adams ought to "have his head taken off."

On a visit to Boston, Adams found that most people ignored him. Exclaimed one Federalist gleefully, "He walks into State Street at the usual hour but seems totally unknown." The senator admitted he was "deserted by my friends, in Boston and in the state legislature." Only on his parents' Quincy farm did he find support for his unpopular action. His father told him, "You have too honest a heart, too independent a mind, and too brilliant talents. . . . My advice to you is . . . to pursue the course you are in. . . . I think it the path of justice."

Even in the face of threats, Senator Adams refused to change his courageous stand on the embargo. Stubbornly he announced his readiness to "sacrifice everything I have in life and even life itself," rather than stop defending the rights of impressed American sailors.

At the end of May 1808 the Federalist legislature in Massachusetts gathered in Boston. The major purpose of their meeting, revealed the governor, was "the political and even the personal destruction of John Quincy Adams." Many months before the proper time for such an election, these bitter men chose James Lloyd, Jr., to take Adams's U.S. Senate seat. Their intended insult was obvious. Though his Senate term lasted another nine months, honor required that John Quincy Adams resign his office. Proud of his accomplishments, he graciously withdrew and returned home to Boston.

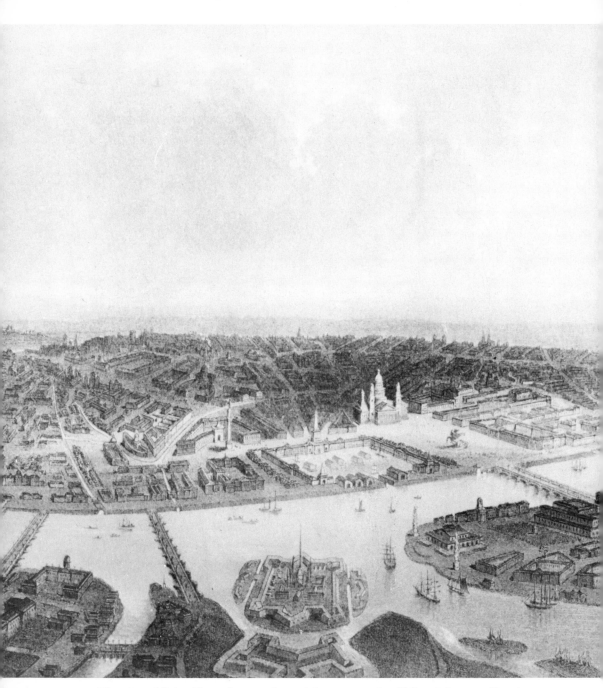

The city of Saint Petersburg, where Adams served as U.S. minister to Russia

Chapter 4

Return to Russia

Without the support of a political party, Adams guessed his public career was at an end. For the next year Adams wrote and delivered lectures as a professor at Harvard and continued his law practice. To relax he spent time gardening. Bent among his flowers and shrubs, Adams perhaps wondered what the future held in store for him.

One important politician recognized Adams's talents, though. Jefferson's secretary of state, James Madison, had become fourth president of the United States on March 4, 1809. Two days later he named John Quincy Adams the first American minister to Russia. Seeing the position as a kind of "honorable diplomatic exile," Adams believed it was his "duty as a citizen to accept the call of country." He was glad to be back in public service.

In August the blue-eyed, five-foot, seven-inch ambassador stood on the deck of the merchant ship *Horace*. His wife Louisa, his youngest son Charles, three secretaries, and two servants were traveling with him on what was now his fourth trip across the Atlantic Ocean to Europe. An eighty-day journey through head winds, fog, and the threat of freezing winter weather at last brought the *Horace* into Saint Petersburg harbor.

In 1809 Saint Petersburg ranked among Europe's grandest cities. Its 400,000 people crowded the cobbled streets, riding in carriages, pulling loaded carts, and selling vegetables from stands. Washington, D.C., with its population of less than 20,000, seemed a crude village by comparison. Russia had never been more powerful. And though the French emperor Napoleon Bonaparte was marching his troops across all of Europe in bloody war, he and Russia had been at peace since 1807.

Settling himself in the capital, Adams remembered many of the sights he had seen as a teenager twenty-seven years before. On November 5, 1809, American Ambassador Adams traveled to the Imperial Palace. Dressed in formal clothes and wearing a wig, he presented himself to the Russian emperor, Alexander I. A true diplomat, Adams told the emperor that the buildings of New York and Philadelphia could not compete with those of Saint Petersburg, "a city of Princes."

A week later Louisa Adams, wearing a hoop dress with a silver-tissue skirt, a long red velvet robe, and a fur cloak, was presented to the emperor's mother. Although handsomely dressed, Louisa could hardly compare with many of the Russian noblewomen she saw. Fancy costumes studded with diamonds and rubies blinded the eye with their glitter. At a splendid ball given by the Russian chancellor, John Quincy Adams observed, "the dresses were more splendid and the profusion of diamonds and other precious stones worn both by the men and women, as well as of ribbons, blue and red, was greater than I ever witnessed anywhere."

While living in Saint Petersburg, Adams often walked along the Neva River. In this scene, the frozen river stretches in front of Saint Isaac's Cathedral, which was built after Adams left the city.

Many of the foreign diplomats in Saint Petersburg entertained in lavish style. The United States government paid Adams too little to throw such parties. He seldom enjoyed staying up so late anyway. "The night parties seldom break up until four or five in the morning," he complained. "It is a life of such irregularity . . . as I cannot and will not continue to lead." As America's ambassador, Adams found another way to show his country's friendliness to the emperor.

For exercise, Adams took a long walk every morning. On October 11, 1810, he recorded in his diary, "As I was walking on the Mall . . . I met the Emperor, who stopped and spoke to me." A month later the same thing happened as Adams ambled along the quay of the Neva River. The emperor, he reported, "asked me what was my habitual walk. I told him commonly to the foundry. He asked where I lived. I told him in the new street, in a corner house, partly fronting on the Moika."

Alexander I, emperor of Russia, was believed to have died in 1825. But when his tomb was opened in 1926, it was empty. Some say he escaped instead to Siberia, where he spent his final years as a monk.

Adams encountered the emperor on other days as well. Strolling together the two chatted about the weather and other everyday matters. But Adams, in this simple, open manner, obtained the emperor's goodwill and soon succeeded in arranging for the Baltic Sea to be opened to American shipping.

Pleased with this achievement, Adams relaxed and enjoyed the unusual Russian customs he observed through the year. On one wintry night he joined a party at the French ambassador's country estate. While servants provided torchlight, ladies and gentlemen took turns sliding down a tall, snow-covered ramp built especially for that purpose. With nothing but his coattails to sit on, it is possible Adams took his turn sailing down this "ice-hill" too.

The Russians' greatest holiday occurred on Easter, and Adams found the custom of giving egg-shaped gifts of particular interest. Peasants presented real eggs, hard-boiled and dyed red, to their masters, for which they received gifts of money. "Persons of higher standing," Adams noted, "present eggs of sugar, glass, giltwood, porcelain, marble, and almost every other substance. . . . Some of these eggs are made to cost a hundred rubles or upwards."

Napoleon Bonaparte and his troops on the march

Suddenly, in April of 1812, Russia's fragile peace with Napoleon abruptly ended. Cannon boomed across the Niemen River on the Russian frontier, and a great French army invaded the countryside, sending the stunned Russian army flying. "Great anxiety here," Adams scribbled in his diary, "rumors of disasters." The American watched as raw Russian troops gathered in Saint Petersburg. "I saw many of them this morning," he remarked, "just in from the country, with the one-horse wagons, and the families of the recruits taking leave of them."

As Napoleon's veteran soldiers pushed eastward, news reached Adams of renewed conflict in the United States. After many years of feuding with the British over the impressment of American sailors, Congress finally declared war against England in June of 1812. This conflict came to be known as the War of 1812. Since Russia and England were allies, Adams's task of maintaining Russia's friendship became delicate.

The burning of Moscow

Throughout the rest of the year, Adams successfully presented America's attitudes to the Russian government. In September the Russians set fire to the city of Moscow, hoping to deprive Napoleon's advancing troops of supplies. With a false sense of triumph French soldiers marched through smoking, empty streets. Napoleon had stretched his men too far. Without supplies, deep in enemy territory, faced with a freezing winter, Napoleon suddenly realized he must retreat. "His race is now run, and his own term of punishment has commenced," predicted Adams. Soon he could report, "From Moscow to Prussia, 800 miles of road have been strewed with his artillery, baggage, wagons, ammunition chests, dead and dying men, whom

Napoleon's disastrous retreat from Moscow

he has been forced to abandon to their fate . . . the two Russian generals who have conquered Napoleon . . . are *General Famine* and *General Frost*." News of further Russian victories rocked the capital. The bells of every church in Saint Petersburg rang the call of glorious victory.

With the collapse of his empire, Napoleon gave up his throne and was forced into exile. As all of Europe returned to peace, the British ended their war with America also. In the spring of 1814, President Madison named John Quincy Adams to lead the peace negotiations with Great Britain. "This opens upon me . . . a new change in the scenery of life," revealed an excited Adams. "The welfare of my family and country . . . are staked upon the event."

Above: The Grand Canal in Ghent, Belgium, where the Treaty of Ghent was signed
Below: A cartoon showing the bear (Russia) urging England (left)
and America (right) to make peace.

Chapter 5

Peacemaker and Diplomat

In June of 1814 Adams arrived in the charming country of Belgium, where the peace talks would be held. Other members of the United States peace commission — Jonathan Russell, James Bayard, Henry Clay, and Albert Gallatin — soon joined him in the city of Ghent. While they waited for the British negotiators to arrive, they tried to enjoy themselves in the small hotel they had rented. Of his comrades, John Quincy Adams sternly complained, "They sit after dinner and drink bad wine and smoke cigars, which neither suits my habits nor my health, and absorbs time which I cannot spare."

Now at the age of forty-seven, John Quincy Adams was short, bald, and stout. His stiff, precise, puritanical manner made him very demanding of others. Just getting along with the other American commissioners required his best diplomatic skills. Henry Clay, for example, was as unlike Adams as any man could be. The tall, thin Kentuckian greatly enjoyed gossip, drinking, and gambling. Rising at dawn one morning, Adams remarked with disgust that he heard a noisy card party just finishing in Clay's room.

Adams's fellow peace commissioners in Ghent:
Henry Clay (left), Albert Gallatin (center), and James Bayard (right)

At last the British negotiators, headed by Lord Gambier, reached Ghent. In August the British and Americans gathered at the Hotel de Pays Bas to begin smoothing out their countries' differences. The British impressment of American seamen no longer remained an issue. With the end of the European war, British sailors themselves could not find enough work. Many other problems did exist, however. Between meetings the Americans and British exchanged letters stating their positions. After writing one such note, Adams watched Clay and the other Americans "sifting, erasing, patching and amending," until Adams's original version seemed hardly recognizable. Still, if it was for the good of the country, Adams was willing to swallow his pride.

The signing of the Treaty of Ghent. Adams shakes hands with Britain's Lord Gambier.

On one matter, though, Adams refused to budge an inch. The British laid claim to Moose Island on the coast of Massachusetts. When Henry Clay and James Bayard urged Adams to give up the island in the name of peace, Adams hotly replied, "Mr. Clay, supposing Moose Island belonged to Kentucky . . . would you give it up as nothing? Mr. Bayard, if it belonged to Delaware, would you?" Finally the men agreed that the issue should be excluded.

On December 24, 1814, the British and American commissioners formally exchanged peace documents. The eight men signed the Treaty of Ghent, bringing the War of 1812 to an end. But even the fastest ship could not bring this news to the United States for several weeks. On January 8, 1815—unaware that a peace treaty had been signed—soldiers fought one last battle in the War of 1812.

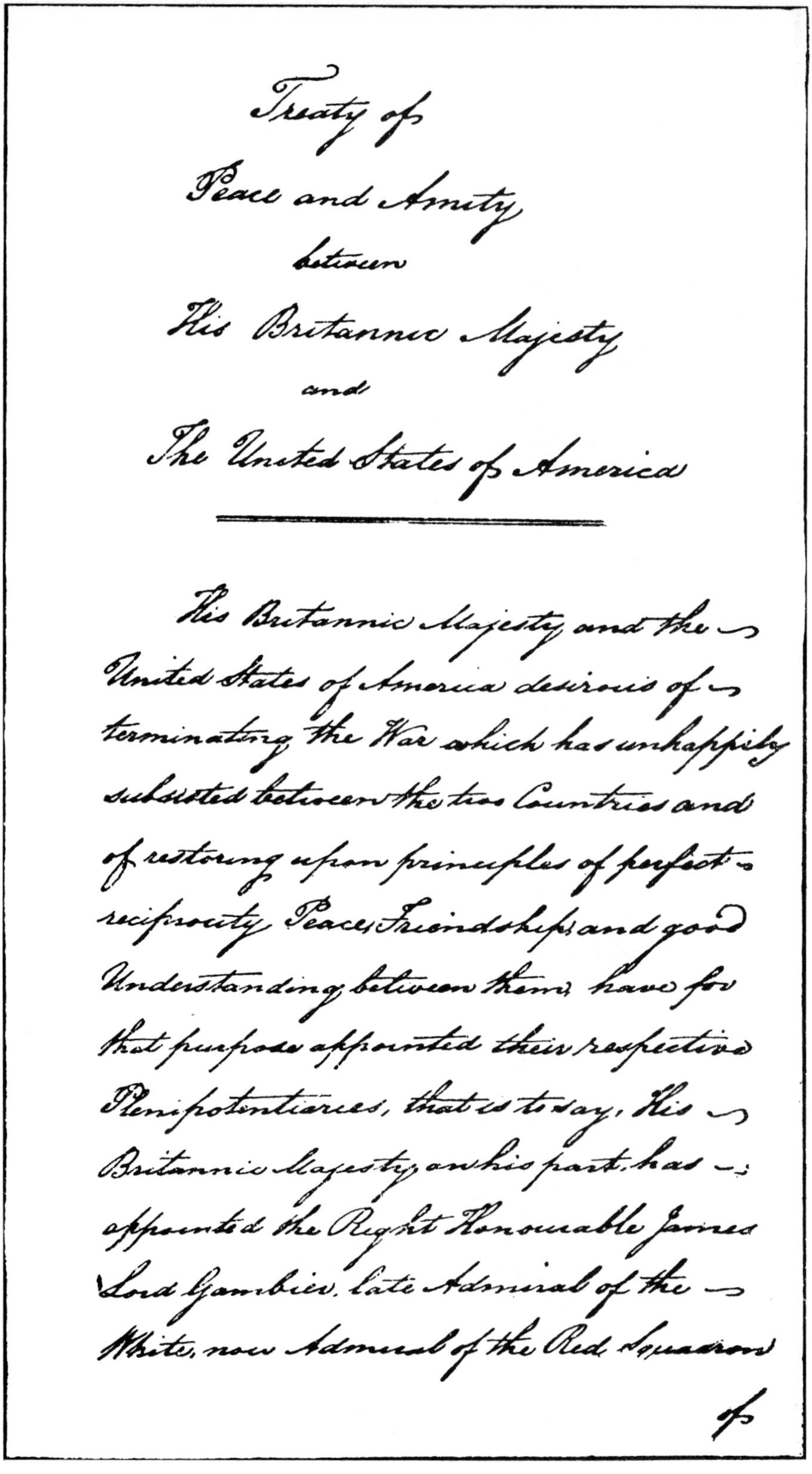

Treaty of

Peace and Amity

between

His Britannic Majesty

and

The United States of America

His Britannic Majesty and the
United States of America desirous of
terminating the War which has unhappily
subsisted between the two Countries and
of restoring upon principles of perfect
reciprocity Peace, Friendship, and good
Understanding between them; have for
that purpose appointed their respective
Plenipotentiaries, that is to say, His
Britannic Majesty on his part, has
appointed the Right Honourable James
Lord Gambier, late Admiral of the
White, now Admiral of the Red Squadron

of

The first page of the Treaty of Ghent

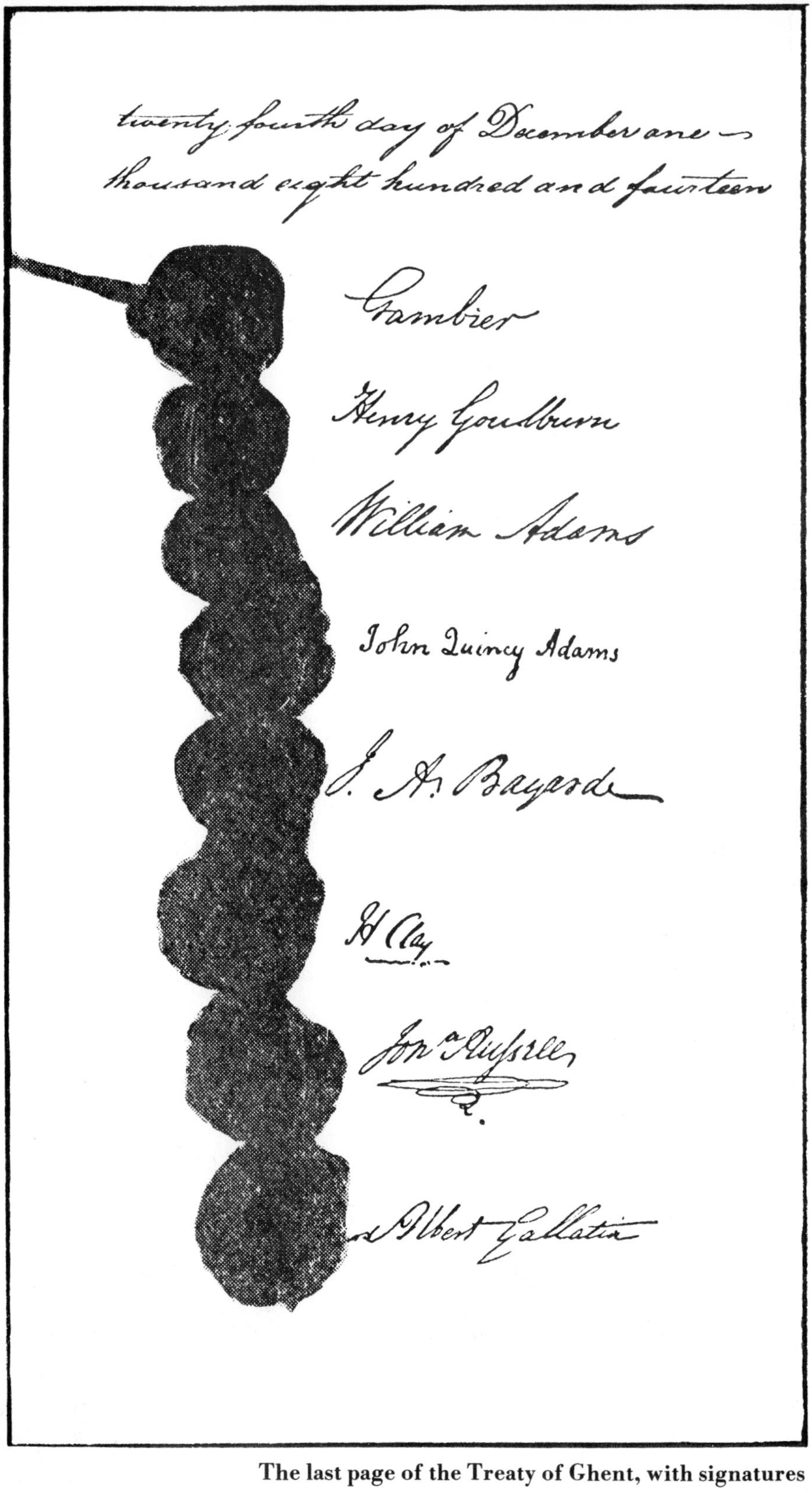

twenty fourth day of December one
thousand eight hundred and fourteen

Gambier

Henry Goulburn

William Adams

John Quincy Adams

J. A. Bayard

H Clay

Jon. Russell

Albert Gallatin

The last page of the Treaty of Ghent, with signatures

Above: Andrew Jackson's troops surprise the British at the Battle of New Orleans. Below: A notice in a New York newspaper announcing the Treaty of Ghent, which ended the War of 1812

Mercantile Advertiser
EXTRA.

New-York, Saturday Evening,

9 o'clock, Feb. 11.

PEACE.

The great and joyful news of PEACE between the United States and Great Britain reached this city this evening by the British sloop of war Favourite, the hon. J. U. Mowatt, Esq. commander, in 42 days from Plymouth.

Henry Carroll, Esq. Secretary of the American Legation at Ghent, is the welcome bearer of the Treaty, which was signed at Ghent on the 24th December, by the respective Commissioners, and ratified by the British government on the 28th of Dez. Mr. Baker, late Secretary to the British Legation at Washington, has also arrived in the sloop of war, with a copy of the Treaty, ratified by the British government.

Both of these gentlemen proceed immediately for the seat of government.

We understand the Treaty is highly honorable to our country.

The Favourite sailed from Plymouth on the 21 day of January and has brought London papers to the 31st December.

Mr. Hughes, one of our Secretaries sailed in the Transit, from Bordeaux for the U. States on the 30th Dec.

Our Ministers were to remain in Europe until spring.

We learn verbally that the Congress at Vienna had not finished their important business.

We understand that London letters of Dec. 31 represent the affairs of the Continent to be yet unsettled.

From the London Courier of Dec. 31.

PARIS, DEC. 27.

The Duke of Wellington received last night the important intelligence of the signing of a TREATY OF PEACE between the British and American Commissioners at Ghent, on the 24th of December. The Courier adds, that no comments were made on this important subject in the Paris Moniteur.

At New Orleans, with blaring bagpipes and booming drums, brave British troops marched into the deadly gunfire of hidden Tennessee and Kentucky militiamen. The one-sided American victory of that day filled the American people with unbounded pride. Overnight General Andrew Jackson, who had commanded the American troops, became a national hero. When news of the Treaty of Ghent arrived fast on the heels of the Battle of New Orleans, the United States erupted with double celebrations. From city to town, church bells rang and cheering crowds overflowed the streets.

Having concluded his duties as a peace commissioner, "the most memorable period of my life," as he put it, John Quincy Adams traveled next to Paris. There he revisited many happy scenes of his boyhood visit and awaited the arrival of his wife and son from Russia. While in Paris, Adams witnessed the return of Napoleon Bonaparte from exile. Thousands of Frenchmen lined the streets shouting, "Long live the emperor! Long live Napoleon!" as he entered the city in triumph and seized control again. England and its European allies reawakened to the threat of war. Not until June would Napoleon be stopped once and for all at the Battle of Waterloo.

While observing these turbulent European affairs, John Quincy Adams received a dispatch in May 1815 naming him minister to Great Britain. Taking up this important post, Adams proudly followed in the footsteps of his father. Many years later, during the American Civil War, John Quincy's son Charles would serve in the same distinguished position.

A portrait of John Quincy Adams

While ambassador to Great Britain, Adams attended royal weddings, balls, and other state functions at Saint James Palace. He preferred, however, to spend his time in the comfort of his charming rented house. At "Little Boston," as he called it, Adams's two oldest sons, George and John, rejoined the family after living with relatives in Massachusetts for many years. Their good performance at English schools led John Quincy to write to his father, "I am happy to assure you that the Yankee boys have done no dishonor to the reputation of their country."

James Monroe is inaugurated as fifth president of the United States.

When James Monroe of Virginia was elected fifth president of the United States in 1816, he was determined to appoint cabinet members who represented the different regions of the country. For the position of secretary of state he sought New England's most experienced man in foreign affairs. Soon John Quincy received a letter from President Monroe informing him, "Respect for your talents and patriotic services has induced me to commit to your care . . . the Department of State."

"London farewell!" wrote Adams not long after. In June 1817, he and his family set sail for New York. It was Adams's eighth crossing of the Atlantic Ocean, and after an absence of eight years he returned once and for all to the United States.

John Quincy Adams
(above) served as
secretary of state
for fifth president
James Monroe (right)

Chapter 6

Secretary of State

September 1817 found the new secretary of state taking up his duties in Washington. With the help of his little staff of eight clerks, Adams interviewed dozens of office seekers and answered stacks of mail.

James Monroe heavily relied on his department heads for advice. At regular cabinet meetings he posed important national questions for them to answer. The carefully reasoned opinions of Secretary of State John Quincy Adams were a great help to President Monroe, whose years in office came to be called the "Era of Good Feeling." As Adams's reputation as a statesman grew, one Washington citizen, George Waterton, observed, "There is no public character in the United States, that has more intellectual power."

Adams had ample opportunities to show his many skills. In 1817 and 1818, rampaging Seminole Indians were attacking and murdering American settlers in southern Georgia. After each raid these Indians took refuge in hidden camps among the Florida swamps. The Florida territory belonged to Spain, so it was foreign soil where Americans could not chase after them.

Indian chiefs captured during the Seminole War

Finally, President Monroe authorized General Andrew Jackson to cross the border into Florida and take command of what came to be known as the Seminole War. Jackson raised an army of Tennessee militia and, in the spring of 1818, angry settlers got their revenge at last. They hunted the Seminoles without mercy. The smoke of burning Indian villages filled the sky. General Jackson also seized several Spanish forts, insisting that if the Spanish could not control the Indians then Americans would.

In Washington the shocked Spanish ambassador, Don Luis de Onis, demanded that Jackson give up the Spanish forts and be punished for his actions. At a hurried meeting, cabinet members discussed the invasion of Florida. President Monroe and all his advisors argued against General Jackson. Only Secretary Adams defended his behavior. Jackson's activities, he privately stated, "were justified by the necessity of the case, and by the misconduct of the Spanish commanding officers in Florida. . . .

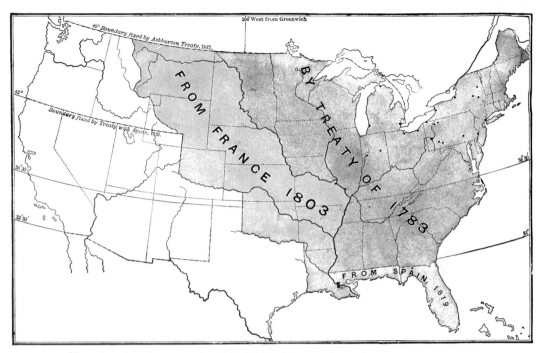

Map showing the growth of the United States through various treaties

Our frontiers could not be protected while the Indians could have safe refuge in Florida." To settle the problem once and for all, Adams began negotiations with Spain to procure the Florida territory for the United States.

On February 22, 1819, Secretary of State Adams and Spanish Ambassador Onis signed a treaty in which Spain ceded Florida to the United States. In return, the U.S. agreed to pay to American citizens the $5 million worth of damages they claimed against Spain because of the Indian raids. "It was," exclaimed Adams, "perhaps, the most important day of my life." This treaty also settled the western border of the Louisiana Territory. A recent British agreement had defined the Canadian border. So now, except for problems with the Maine and Oregon borders, the United States possessed a definite boundary line all the way to the Pacific Ocean.

The country's expanding borders caused a major crisis in 1820. Eager to settle new lands, pioneers scrambled into the Missouri territory west of the Mississippi River. By 1820 enough people lived in this fertile region to apply for statehood.

Since the beginning of the Union, Southern slave-holding states shared equal representation with the nonslavery states of the North. But when Missouri applied for statehood in 1819, Congressman James Talmadge of New York suggested that Missouri be admitted as a nonslavery or "free-soil" state.

Many people believed this would upset the delicate balance of power. When Representative Rufus King of New York spoke out against slavery, Secretary Adams observed, "the great slave-holders in the House gnawed their lips and clenched their fists as they heard him. . . . The slave-holders cannot hear" his speeches "without being seized with cramps." Across the Capitol hall in the Senate, Southerners openly grumbled about quitting the Union to protect their way of life. All other business in Washington ground to a halt while the issue was debated.

Finally Senator Jesse Thomas of Illinois suggested a compromise. The new state of Maine would be admitted as a free state while Missouri would be allowed into the Union as a slave state. The balance would remain: twelve slave states in the South and twelve free states in the North. Thereafter, however, no new slave state could be admitted above an imaginary line drawn along the southern Missouri border.

The slavery issue eventually broke America in two.

When the Missouri Compromise reached President Monroe's desk, Secretary Adams counseled him to sign the bill, since no better solution could be found. In his diary Adams insisted, however, that "Slavery is the great and foul stain upon the North American Union. . . . If the Union must be dissolved, slavery is precisely the question upon which it ought to break." Clearly Adams saw the problem that forty years later would lead to America's Civil War.

On a day-to-day basis, the public requirements of his office filled more of John Quincy's time than he wished. Regretfully he wrote, "Visitors at the office occupied . . . all the hours of business. . . . Every man comes with a story. . . almost everyone comes to ask favors. No sooner has one left the office than another enters." Listening to these people kept Adams from more important work, causing him to protest, "The sun goes down upon business uncompleted."

Among Adams's various duties were all the government's dealings with foreign countries, preparations for the 1820 census, and a study to standardize the nation's system of weights and measures. In a letter to his father he complained, "I am handcuffed by Spain, fettered with the census, and chained to the floor with a load of Weights and Measures."

Actually Adams enjoyed the important nature of his job. Gladly he served the country in any way he could. With intelligence and stubbornness he defended the rights of the United States. On one occasion British ambassador Stratford Canning burst into Adams's office. The Englishman had heard about American settlements at the mouth of the Columbia River in the disputed Oregon Territory. He paced the room in a rage, complaining that the United States had no right to be there.

"Have you any *claim* to the mouth of the Columbia River?" cut in John Quincy Adams at last.

"Why," exclaimed Canning, "do you not *know* that we have a claim?"

"I do not *know* what you claim nor what you do not claim," retorted Adams. "You claim India; you claim Africa; you claim—"

"Perhaps a piece of the moon," rudely interrupted Canning.

"No," answered Adams with dignity, "I have not heard that you claim . . . any part of the moon; but there is not a spot on *this* globe that . . . you do not claim."

When Adams refused to back down from his views, the Englishman silently left the office.

Settlers clear the American wilderness.

In 1820 James Monroe easily won reelection as president. At the meeting of the electoral college, only one delegate voted against him. That single vote went to John Quincy Adams. (A New Hampshire delegate had voted for Adams so that George Washington would remain the only president to have been elected by a unanimous vote.)

The "Era of Good Feeling" continued into President Monroe's second term. The country prospered as settlers cut farms out of the nation's wilderness and the thumping of factory machinery announced the production of valued American goods. As the United States grew, it began to feel its strength.

Left: Simón Bolívar, called the "George Washington of South America"
Right: José de San Martín, South American soldier and statesman

The major event of these years was the announcement of the Monroe Doctrine, which Secretary Adams helped to write. In South America, Generals Simón Bolívar, José de San Martín, and others were leading revolutionaries in a great fight for freedom against Spanish rule. By 1822 Monroe urged Congress to recognize the independence of Colombia, Chile, Peru, Mexico, and Argentina. United States citizens, caught up in the excitement, demanded that Spain give up its claims to these territories.

At cabinet meetings, John Quincy Adams strongly advised the president to regard further "interference on the part of the European powers and especially an attack on the Colonies by them, as an attack on ourselves." President Monroe instructed Adams to begin drafting such a statement. Meanwhile, Britain was urging the United States to join with them in warning the Europeans to keep out of the Americas. But Adams insisted that the U.S. act alone. Monroe took his advice.

James Monroe discusses the Monroe Doctrine with his cabinet

On December 3, 1823, in his annual message to Congress, President Monroe warned the European powers that the United States "should consider any attempt on their part to extend their system to any portion of this hemisphere as dangerous to our peace and safety." Our country had never entangled itself in European affairs. Now Monroe insisted that Europe must not interfere with the independent nations of the Western Hemisphere, unless it wished to risk war with the United States.

News of the presidential message spread quickly. From Stockholm, American Christopher Hughes revealed it was "the exclusive topick of European conversation, and has attracted all eyes to our Hemisphere." It would be some time yet before European nations thought of the U.S. as a powerful country. But with the Monroe Doctrine the United States had begun to win respect.

Chapter 7

President of the United States

As the presidential election of 1824 neared, Secretary of the Treasury William Crawford and Secretary of War John C. Calhoun revealed their desire to be president. Other strong candidates were Henry Clay, now a Kentucky congressman, and the new senator from Tennessee, General Andrew Jackson.

New England's politicians clamored for a candidate of their own. They urged the country's foremost statesman, John Quincy Adams, to begin lining up political support. Steadfastly Adams refused them, insisting, "I only want what is freely bestowed."

Adams himself did not expect to become president. His enemies, however, attacked him anyway. One newspaper printed a claim that Adams never wore a waistcoat or a cravat and sometimes walked to church barefoot. Adams denied these crude charges, admitting only that on very hot days he wore "a black silk riband" around his neck instead of the traditional cravat.

Opposite page: A ball given by Mrs. Adams at the White House. Adams is on the left and Jackson is in the center.

An 1824 cartoon showing Adams, Crawford, and Jackson getting ready to race for the presidency. Henry Clay scratches his head (right).

Some newspapers made fun of Adams's severe personality. Even an Adams supporter was forced to admit the secretary seemed "hard as a piece of granite and cold as a lump of ice." Adams complained, "I am wearied of hearing the name of Adams treated with so little respect and ceremony." But he, too, recognized his weaknesses, stating, "I am a man of reserved, cold, austere, and forbidding manners." People found it difficult to become friends with John Quincy Adams. Yet those who appreciated his patriotism and talented statesmanship wanted him to be president.

Soon John C. Calhoun dropped out of the presidential race to run for vice-president instead. When William Crawford suffered a serious illness Adams's chances further improved. Still, Andrew Jackson, the popular "Hero of New Orleans," possessed tremendous support in the southern and western states.

In November 1824, along America's city streets and country roads, voters traveled to the polls. They voted for presidential electors who in turn would vote for the president. A candidate needed 131 electoral votes to win. For days officials across the nation counted the paper ballots, and when the votes were finally tallied the results were:

	Popular Vote	Electoral Vote
Andrew Jackson	153,544	99
John Quincy Adams	108,740	84
William Crawford	46,618	41
Henry Clay	47,136	37

No candidate had received a clear majority. Therefore, according to the Constitution, the House of Representatives would choose the president from the top three men.

Forced out of the contest, Henry Clay realized he possessed tremendous political power. As Speaker of the House, he had many supporters in Congress. By throwing his support to either Jackson or Adams, he could influence the election's result. On January 9, 1825, John Quincy Adams reported in his diary, "Mr. Clay came at six, and spent the evening with me in a long conversation." Of the upcoming House vote, Clay "had no hesitation in saying that his preference would be for me."

On February 9, 1825, excited congressmen climbed the snowy Capitol steps and entered the House of Representatives. Curious citizens jammed the galleries, almost pouring over the railings. With the votes of Clay's supporters, Adams appeared to have a clear advantage. And if he carried New York it seemed he would surely triumph.

New York's delegation was evenly split between Crawford and Adams. Only Congressman Stephen Van Rensselaer wavered. As the wooden voting box neared him, the old man closed his eyes and prayed for guidance. Upon opening them he saw before all else an Adams ballot lying on the floor. He picked it up and put it in the box. This simple, fateful act elected John Quincy Adams president of the United States. While Jackson took the votes of seven states and Crawford the votes of four, Adams with the New York vote carried a majority of thirteen.

Completely surprised but grateful, Adams prepared to become the sixth president. Soon his political opponents were yelling about a "corrupt bargain" when he named Henry Clay secretary of state. They claimed Adams sold that office to Clay in exchange for his support. In spite of their stinging protest, however, Adams refused to change his mind. He truly believed that Clay was the best man for the job.

A curious crowd packed the street in front of the Adams house on the morning of March 4, 1825. They cheered when at 11:30 they saw John Quincy Adams step outside and climb into his carriage. Next the people glimpsed President Monroe, following behind in a second carriage, about to perform his last official act. An escort of uniformed militia proudly marched along with the two carriages as they rolled forward to the Capitol.

Finally entering the House of Representatives, thronged with congressmen, ladies, and foreign diplomats, fifty-seven-year-old John Quincy Adams prepared to give his inaugural speech. The knowledge that only one-third of

John Marshall, chief justice of the Supreme Court from 1801 to 1835

the people had actually voted for him made Adams humble and nervous. Standing beside the speaker's chair, he addressed his listeners: "I am deeply conscious of the prospect that I shall stand more and oftener in need of your indulgence." He assured the people, however, that his intentions were "upright and pure." He would enter upon the duties of the presidency with "a heart devoted to the welfare of the country."

Adams's speech finished, John Marshall, chief justice of the Supreme Court, stepped forward to administer the oath of office. With his hand upon a book of laws, Adams promised "to the best of my ability, to preserve, protect, and defend the Constitution of the United States."

Ex-president Monroe and other important politicians approached to shake Adams's hand. In front of the Capitol, military companies paraded in smart review for the new commander-in-chief. Escorted home again, Adams greeted visitors who came to wish him well. In the evening he watched elegantly dressed gentlemen dance with brightly gowned ladies at the crowded inaugural ball.

The President's Mansion

In April Adams and his family moved into the huge, drafty President's Mansion, already called the White House by the common people. Once settled, President Adams kept up a busy daily schedule. Most mornings he arose about five o'clock and went out to get some exercise. "I walk by the light of the moon or stars . . . about four miles," he revealed, "usually returning home in time to see the sun rise." After lighting a fire, he would read the Bible and the newspapers. As soon as he finished breakfast, an endless line of visitors called upon him. Some had genuine business. Others were simply curious. A few begged for charity. "The department heads of course," he remarked, "occupy much of this time." Late in the afternoon he would stop for dinner and, unless he entertained company, he spent the evening reading and signing government papers. At about eleven o'clock he retired to bed and ended his day.

A dinner party during John Quincy Adams's presidency

Always an active man, on hot summer mornings President Adams sometimes went swimming naked in the Potomac River. Though an excellent swimmer, this habit caused him trouble on occasion. One morning while he swam, someone stole his clothes from the riverbank. Luckily, a passing boy helped him by running to the White House to get him some others. Another day he expected to paddle across the river in a canoe and swim back. But water poured into the leaky canoe until it sank. In the water, President Adams gasped for air and struggled for his life. The loose sleeves of his shirt filled with water and "hung like two fifty-six pound weights" upon his arms. With difficulty he reached the shore at last. But the loss of much of his clothing in the river forced him to return to the White House "half dressed."

On another day while Adams swam alone, a Washington newspaperwoman named Anne Royall arrived on the riverbank.

"Come here!" she called out.

"What do you want?" answered Adams in surprise.

"I'm Anne Royall," she snapped. "I've been trying to see you to get an interview out of you for months. . . . I'm sitting on your clothes and you don't get them till I get the interview."

"Let me get out and dress," pleaded Adams.

When she refused, his only choice was to give her the interview while he stood up to his chin in the water.

During his term as president, John Quincy Adams pushed many ambitious plans for "the benefit of the people." With money gained through the careful sale of public lands, Adams urged the establishment of a national university as well as a naval academy. He proposed the building of an astronomical observatory to examine the stars and the construction of roads and canals to stimulate national commerce. "The spirit of improvement is abroad upon the earth," he predicted.

Unfortunately, the members of Congress fought Adams and his projects every step of the way. Without the support of the people, few of the president's lofty ideas were ever acted upon. Depressed by his constant failures, Adams found the presidency a "harassing, wearying, teasing condition of existence."

Among Adams's many political enemies were those who still believed that he and Henry Clay had cheated to win the election. In the spring of 1826, Virginia congressman

Congressman
John Randolph

John Randolph took the floor in the House of Representatives. For hours he ranted against both Adams and Clay, finally insisting that Clay was nothing more than a "blackleg."

In the American slang of that day, a blackleg was a swindler or dishonest gambler. Stung by this insult Secretary of State Clay challenged Randolph to a duel. On the afternoon of April 8, 1826, the two men met on the Virginia side of the Potomac River. Standing at a distance of ten paces they fired pistols at one another. Randolph's whizzing bullet struck a stump behind Clay. Clay's bullet tore a hole through the lower part of Congressman Randolph's coat. Fortunately a second exchange of gunfire caused no injury either. The affair having "ended in smoke" and nothing worse, the secretary of state left the dueling ground feeling his honor was restored.

Celebrating the Fourth of July

The summer of 1826 found Americans making special plans to celebrate Independence Day. That Fourth of July marked the fiftieth anniversary of the signing of the Declaration of Independence. To honor the day, joyful citizens shot off fireworks, marched in parades, and threw logs on great bonfires. In Quincy, Massachusetts, people shouted the toast that old John Adams, a signer of the Declaration, offered for the occasion: "Independence Forever!"

Few people realized the ninety-one-year-old patriot lay close to death that very day. Family and doctors around his bedside tried to make him comfortable. When told it was the Fourth of July, John Adams answered, "It is a great day. It is a good day." Later he breathed with difficulty, "Thomas Jefferson survives." These were his dying words. Little did he know that these words were not true.

**Thomas Jefferson (above) and
John Adams (right) both died
on the Fourth of July, 1826,
the fiftieth anniversary of the
Declaration of Independence.**

Earlier that day at Monticello, his Virginia estate, eighty-three-year-old Thomas Jefferson, the writer of the Declaration of Independence, also lay very ill. Rousing himself from a faint he asked, "This is the Fourth?" When told it was, he sighed, "Just as I wished." Sinking back on his pillow, he died, just a few hours before Adams.

As news of these deaths reached people across the country, they shook their heads in wonder. That two such great Americans should die on the same important day seemed an unusual twist of fate. Saddened to learn about his father, John Quincy Adams revealed, "For myself all that I dare to ask is, that I may live the remnant of my days in a manner worthy of him."

The Marquis de Lafayette laying the cornerstone of the Bunker Hill Monument during his tour of the United States

Though Adams believed his time as president was filled with "crazing cares," the United States thrived while he was in office. A visit in 1825 by a great patriot of the American Revolution, the French Marquis de Lafayette, filled the nation with pride and thanks. Making a grand tour of the United States, the "boy general" of the Revolution was now a poor old man. With gratitude Americans remembered, though, all he had done for the country. As Lafayette traveled through all twenty-four states, cheering crowds greeted him everywhere with banquets and parades. Children wore ribbons in his honor. Old war veterans stepped up and shook his hand. Aware of his poverty, Congress voted to give the general $200,000 and a large piece of Florida property. At a White House reception President Adams told him, "In your visit . . . you have heard the mingled voices of the past, the present and the future age, joining in one universal chorus of delight at your approach. . . . We shall look upon you always as belonging to us." Teary-eyed, the Frenchman hugged the president.

The United States that Lafayette saw in 1825 was very different than the one for which he had fought so many years before. The thriving young nation was growing stronger every day. The great Erie Canal showed best what Americans could do when they put their minds to it. Winding 363 miles across New York from Lake Erie to the Hudson River, thousands of workmen toiled eight years digging the Erie Canal. When they finished in 1825, they had created an important link between the eastern and western states. While the many goods of New England's booming factories flowed west on canal boats, the farm products and raw materials of Ohio, Indiana, Illinois, and other states poured eastward.

The spirit of progress excited Americans. United States merchant ships carried news of the country's good fortune to European ports. By 1827 thousands of poor Irishmen and Germans flocked to America in search of opportunity. These cheap laborers helped the nation grow even faster.

Unfortunately, as white settlers pushed westward in search of new farmlands, the native Indians suffered. In Georgia, peaceful Cherokees were forced to give up their lands when greedy farmers broke old treaties and marched onto the reservations. In Michigan Territory, Winnebago Indians fought a brief war to stop the advance of the white settlers. By 1828, however, they too were forced to surrender their territorial rights.

Above: The construction of the Erie Canal. Below: New York governor DeWitt Clinton empties Lake Erie water into the Atlantic Ocean in the canal opening ceremony.

The Erie Canal revolutionized transportation in the northern part of the country.

PRESIDENCY!!!

This is the House that We built.

TREASURY.

This is the malt that lay in the House that WE Built,

John Q. Adams,

This is the *MAIDEN* all forlorn, who worried herself from night till morn, to enter the House that We built.

CLAY,

This is the *MAN* all tattered and torn, who courted the maiden all forlorn, who worried herself from night till morn to enter the House that We built.

WEBSTER,

This is the *PRIEST*, all shaven and shorn, that married the man all tattered and torn, unto the maiden all forlorn, who worried herself from night till morn, to enter the House that We Built.

CONGRESS,

This is the BEAST, that carried the Priest all shaven and shorn, who married the man all tattered and torn, unto the maiden all forlorn, who worried herself from night till morn, to enter the House that We Built.

CABINET,

These are the *Rats* that pulled off their hats, and joined the Beast that carried the Priest all shaven and shorn, who married the man all tattered and torn, unto the maiden all forlorn who worried herself from night till morn to enter the House that We built.

"OLD HICKORY,"

This is the *Wood*, well season'd and good, We will use as a rod to whip out the RATS, that pulled off their hats and joined the Beast that carried the Priest all shaven and shorn, who married the man all tattered and torn, unto the maiden all forlorn, who worried herself from night till morn, to enter the House that We Built

NEW-YORK.

This is the *state*, both early and late, that will strengthen the Wood well seasoned and good, to be used as a rod to whip out Rats that pulled off their hats, and joined the beast that carried the Priest all shaven and shorn, who married the man all tattered and torn unto the maiden all forlorn, who worried herself from night till morn to enter the House that We Built.

EBONY & TOPAZ.

• *The People.*

Chapter 8

To Fall and Rise Again

During the years of Adams's presidency two new political parties began to take shape. The old Democratic-Republican party, formed under Thomas Jefferson, was split between Adams followers and Jackson followers. The Adams people came to be called National Republicans, while Jackson's kept the name Democratic Republicans. By the fall of 1828 these two parties were locked in a bitter political contest. Believing Andrew Jackson should have been elected four years earlier, the Democratic-Republicans were determined to make him president now.

Pamphlets, newspapers, and handbills reminded the public of the "corrupt bargain" of 1824. At public meetings, speakers called Adams a snob who hated the people. "King John the Second" they labeled him, claiming he stole money from the public treasury, filled the White House with expensive furniture, and bought a billiard table for gambling purposes. Greatly saddened, Adams felt that these awful rumors left his "character and reputation a wreck."

Opposite page: A Jackson campaign poster

This 1828 cartoon shows Adams men forcing a voter to vote for Adams.

Adams's supporters fought back by attacking Andrew Jackson. They charged Jackson with being a murderer and a slave trader. They dredged up old stories of his youthful gambling and his ferocious brawling. They even made fun of his wife, Rachel, a simple country woman who sometimes smoked a corncob pipe.

Well-organized Jackson men held parades and barbecues to honor "Old Hickory," as Jackson was nicknamed. In town squares, campaigners erected tall hickory poles, and around late-night bonfires they shouted the praises of the "Hero of New Orleans."

John Quincy Adams's campaigners were less effective. Always stiff and formal, President Adams failed to arouse the public's imagination the way Andrew Jackson did. After four years of frustration as president, Adams prepared himself for failure on election day of 1828.

By early December, after days of uncertainty, the final election results reached Washington:

	Popular Vote	Electoral Vote
Andrew Jackson	647,276	178
John Quincy Adams	508,064	83

Andrew Jackson's supporters had swept Adams out of office in a landslide. Though Adams carried the New England states, as well as Delaware, New Jersey, and parts of Maryland and New York, Jackson took every southern and western state.

Embarrassed by the size of his defeat, Adams wrote, "The sun of my political life sets in the deepest gloom."

After such an ugly campaign, Adams refused to attend Jackson's presidential inauguration on March 4, 1829. On that sunny day huge crowds of farmers and frontiersmen packed Pennsylvania Avenue. They strained to see frail, white-haired Jackson as he rode from the Capitol in victory toward the White House.

Perhaps the echos of their cheers drifted several miles to John Quincy Adams's temporary home, Meridian Hill. Sitting in despair, Adams remarked, "I can yet scarcely realize my situation." Soon he would return to Massachusetts "to go into the deepest retirement and withdraw from all connections with public affairs."

The Adamses' Quincy mansion

At the "Old House" in Quincy, which he inherited from his father, Adams spent idle hours reading and gardening. Gloomily he believed, "My whole life has been a succession of disappointments. I can scarcely recollect a single instance of success to anything that I ever undertook." Then in August of 1830 a committee of local politicians asked if he would be willing to run for a seat in the House of Representatives. They hesitated to ask the ex-president to serve in such a lowly position. Nevertheless, excited at the idea of going back to work, Adams told them, "No person could be degraded by serving the people as a Representative in Congress. Nor, in my opinion, would an ex-President of the United States be degraded by serving as a selectman of his town, if elected thereto by the people."

In November the citizens of the Plymouth district voted overwhelmingly to make John Quincy Adams their representative. "No election or appointment conferred upon me ever gave me so much pleasure," the old man exclaimed. At the age of sixty-three Adams returned to Washington with renewed energy. Greeting him with a smile, his old friend Henry Clay, also a new congressman, asked Adams how it felt to be a boy again.

Above: A photograph of John Quincy Adams as an old man

Chapter 9

Old Man Eloquent

On December 5, 1831, Adams took seat number 23 in the House of Representatives and began his duties as a congressman. When warned that the work would be difficult, Adams answered, "I well know this, but labor I shall not refuse, so long as my hands, my eyes, and my brain, do not desert me."

During his next seventeen years as a congressman, Adams took part in all of the major issues brought before the Congress. But nothing he did was more important than his fight against the hated "gag rule."

On his first day in Congress, Adams presented fifteen petitions calling for an end to slavery and the slave trade in the District of Columbia. Angry Southerners soon saw that the right to petition Congress in this way endangered their way of life. In May of 1836 Southern congressmen forced the passing of the gag rule, which insisted that "All petitions . . . relating in any way . . . to the subject of slavery . . . shall . . . be laid on the table, and that no further action whatever shall be had thereon."

John Quincy Adams in Congress defending the right to petition

With all his energy, John Quincy Adams fought against the gag rule. At first it seemed every man in Congress opposed him, the Southerners were so powerful. "Wind and tide are against me on this subject," admitted Adams.

Still the old gentleman would never quit the fight. At every opportunity he jumped to his feet in the House to offer new petitions. "While a remnant of physical power is left me to write and speak," he promised, "the world will retire from me before I shall retire from the world." On a visit to the House of Representatives, the English writer Charles Dickens observed, "Adams is a fine old fellow . . . with the most surprising vigour, memory, readiness, and pluck."

A picture from an English children's book showing two children
presenting a petition to abolish the slave trade

As Adams slowly gained Northern support for his
views, the slaveholders of the South grew to hate him
more. Among the death threats he received, one letter con-
tained his picture with the mark of a rifle ball on his
forehead. Beneath it a motto read, "To stop the music of
John Quincy Adams, sixth President of the United States,

> Who, in the space of one revolving moon
> Is statesman, poet, babbler, and buffoon."

Such threats only spurred Adams to fight harder for
what he knew was right. As time passed, many Americans

recognized Adams as a hero in the cause of freedom of speech. Finally, in 1844, enough congressmen agreed with him to overturn the gag rule at last. No moment in his long career could have given John Quincy Adams more pleasure.

In his old age as a congressman, Adams kept fighting for his beliefs. He voted against the annexation of Texas and tried to stop the involvement of the United States in its war with Mexico. He knew these actions would only hasten the growth of slavery in the American Southwest and increase the problem that would one day break the United States in two.

On November 20, 1846, Adams suddenly toppled over while walking on a Boston street. The mild stroke he suffered that day kept him in bed for several months. As soon as he recovered, he insisted on returning to the House of Representatives.

As he entered the chamber, all business halted. Congressmen rose to greet him and two of them escorted him to his seat. They were glad to have the congressman they called "Old Man Eloquent" back.

For the next full year John Quincy Adams could be found dutifully working at his desk. At every roll call, members heard his loud yes or no. On February 21, 1848, eighty-year-old Adams attended Congress as usual. During a vote on the treaty of peace with Mexico, the faithful old man suddenly clutched at the corner of his desk and slumped over.

"Mr. Adams is dying!" shouted Congressman Washington Hunt of New York.

Adams suffers a stroke in the House of Representatives.

In alarm, Congressman Davis Fisher of Ohio moved fast enough to catch Adams in his arms before he fell to the floor. Stunned congressmen watched as others placed Adams on a sofa and carried him into the Speaker's chamber. Henry Clay stood close at hand, weeping for his comrade. It seemed this second stroke would surely kill the old man. For a few moments Adams revived, long enough to murmur, "This is the last of earth: I am content."

John Quincy Adams on his deathbed

For the next two days he lay in a coma in the Speaker's chamber. But on the evening of February 23, 1848, John Quincy Adams finally gave up his last battle and died in the Capitol.

All the nation mourned the death of its most dedicated public servant. Thousands of people, Northerners and Southerners alike, filed past his coffin while he lay in state in the Capitol. No one could ever doubt that John Quincy Adams had loved his country. Even his enemies came forward now to do him honor.

"Where could death have found him," proclaimed Senator Thomas Hart Benton of Missouri, "but at the post of duty."

Isaac E. Holmes of South Carolina stated, "When a great man falls, the nation mourns; when a patriarch is removed, the people weep."

Congress erected this monument in Quincy, Massachusetts, to honor
John Adams and his son John Quincy Adams.

Americans had grown used to John Quincy Adams.
From the time of the American Revolution onward he had
always been there, helping the nation along in any way he
could. "Born a citizen of Massachusetts. Died a citizen of
the United States," read the banner over the door of
Boston's Faneuil Hall where Adams's body was taken next
for viewing. In another few days he lay buried in Quincy,
Massachusetts, near his father in the family's churchyard
tomb. "Old Man Eloquent" lay at rest at last. But his fiery
spirit, his loyalty, and his countless contributions to the
United States would never be forgotten.

Chronology of American History

(Shaded area covers events in John Quincy Adams's lifetime.)

About A.D. 982—Eric the Red, born in Norway, reaches Greenland in one of the first European voyages to North America.

About 1000—Leif Ericson (Eric the Red's son) leads what is thought to be the first European expedition to mainland North America; Leif probably lands in Canada.

1492—Christopher Columbus, seeking a sea route from Spain to the Far East, discovers the New World.

1497—John Cabot reaches Canada in the first English voyage to North America.

1513—Ponce de León explores Florida in search of the fabled Fountain of Youth.

1519-1521—Hernando Cortés of Spain conquers Mexico.

1534—French explorers led by Jacques Cartier enter the Gulf of St. Lawrence in Canada.

1540—Spanish explorer Francisco Coronado begins exploring the American Southwest, seeking the riches of the mythical Seven Cities of Cibola.

1565—St. Augustine, Florida, the first permanent European town in what is now the United States, is founded by the Spanish.

1607—Jamestown, Virginia, is founded, the first permanent English town in the present-day U.S.

1608—Frenchman Samuel de Champlain founds the village of Quebec, Canada.

1609—Henry Hudson explores the eastern coast of present-day U.S. for the Netherlands; the Dutch then claim parts of New York, New Jersey, Delaware, and Connecticut and name the area New Netherland.

1619—The English colonies' first shipment of black slaves arrives in Jamestown.

1620—English Pilgrims found Massachusetts's first permanent town at Plymouth.

1621—Massachusetts Pilgrims and Indians hold the famous first Thanksgiving feast in colonial America.

1623—Colonization of New Hampshire is begun by the English.

1624—Colonization of present-day New York State is begun by the Dutch at Fort Orange (Albany).

1625—The Dutch start building New Amsterdam (now New York City).

1630—The town of Boston, Massachusetts, is founded by the English Puritans.

1633—Colonization of Connecticut is begun by the English.

1634—Colonization of Maryland is begun by the English.

1636—Harvard, the colonies' first college, is founded in Massachusetts. Rhode Island colonization begins when Englishman Roger Williams founds Providence.

1638—Delaware colonization begins as Swedes build Fort Christina at present-day Wilmington.

1640—Stephen Daye of Cambridge, Massachusetts prints *The Bay Psalm Book*, the first English-language book published in what is now the U.S.

1643—Swedish settlers begin colonizing Pennsylvania.

About 1650—North Carolina is colonized by Virginia settlers.

1660—New Jersey colonization is begun by the Dutch at present-day Jersey City.

1670—South Carolina colonization is begun by the English near Charleston.

1673—Jacques Marquette and Louis Jolliet explore the upper Mississippi River for France.

1682—Philadelphia, Pennsylvania, is settled. La Salle explores Mississippi River all the way to its mouth in Louisiana and claims the whole Mississippi Valley for France.

1693—College of William and Mary is founded in Williamsburg, Virginia.

1700—Colonial population is about 250,000.

1703—Benjamin Franklin is born in Boston.

1732—George Washington, first president of the U.S., is born in Westmoreland County, Virginia.

1733—James Oglethorpe founds Savannah, Georgia; Georgia is established as the thirteenth colony.

1735—John Adams, second president of the U.S., is born in Braintree, Massachusetts.

1737—William Byrd founds Richmond, Virginia.

1738—British troops are sent to Georgia over border dispute with Spain.

1739—Black insurrection takes place in South Carolina.

1740—English Parliament passes act allowing naturalization of immigrants to American colonies after seven-year residence.

1743—Thomas Jefferson is born in Albemarle County, Virginia. Benjamin Franklin retires at age thirty-seven to devote himself to scientific inquiries and public service.

1744—King George's War begins; France joins war effort against England.

1745—During King George's War, France raids settlements in Maine and New York.

1747—Classes begin at Princeton College in New Jersey.

1748—The Treaty of Aix-la-Chapelle concludes King George's War.

1749—Parliament legally recognizes slavery in colonies and the inauguration of the plantation system in the South. George Washington becomes the surveyor for Culpepper County in Virginia.

1750—Thomas Walker passes through and names Cumberland Gap on his way toward Kentucky region. Colonial population is about 1,200,000.

1751—James Madison, fourth president of the U.S., is born in Port Conway, Virginia. English Parliament passes Currency Act, banning New England colonies from issuing paper money. George Washington travels to Barbados.

1752—Pennsylvania Hospital, the first general hospital in the colonies, is founded in Philadelphia. Benjamin Franklin uses a kite in a thunderstorm to demonstrate that lightning is a form of electricity.

1753—George Washington delivers command that the French withdraw from the Ohio River Valley; French disregard the demand. Colonial population is about 1,328,000.

1754—French and Indian War begins (extends to Europe as the Seven Years' War). Washington surrenders at Fort Necessity.

1755—French and Indians ambush Braddock. Washington becomes commander of Virginia troops.

1756—England declares war on France.

1758—James Monroe, fifth president of the U.S., is born in Westmoreland County, Virginia.

1759—Cherokee Indian war begins in southern colonies; hostilities extend to 1761. George Washington marries Martha Dandridge Custis.

1760—George III becomes king of England. Colonial population is about 1,600,000.

1762—England declares war on Spain.

1763—Treaty of Paris concludes the French and Indian War and the Seven Years' War. England gains Canada and most other French lands east of the Mississippi River.

1764—British pass the Sugar Act to gain tax money from the colonists. The issue of taxation without representation is first introduced in Boston. John Adams marries Abigail Smith.

1765—Stamp Act goes into effect in the colonies. Business virtually stops as almost all colonists refuse to use the stamps.

1766—British repeal the Stamp Act.

1767—John Quincy Adams, sixth president of the U.S. and son of second president John Adams, is born in Braintree, Massachusetts. Andrew Jackson, seventh president of the U.S., is born in Waxhaw settlement, South Carolina.

1769—Daniel Boone sights the Kentucky Territory.

1770—In the Boston Massacre, British soldiers kill five colonists and injure six. Townshend Acts are repealed, thus eliminating all duties on imports to the colonies except tea.

1771—Benjamin Franklin begins his autobiography, a work that he will never complete. The North Carolina assembly passes the "Bloody Act," which makes rioters guilty of treason.

1772—Samuel Adams rouses colonists to consider British threats to self-government.

1773—English Parliament passes the Tea Act. Colonists dressed as Mohawk Indians board British tea ships and toss 342 casks of tea into the water in what becomes known as the Boston Tea Party. William Henry Harrison is born in Charles City County, Virginia.

1774—British close the port of Boston to punish the city for the Boston Tea Party. First Continental Congress convenes in Philadelphia.

1775—American Revolution begins with battles of Lexington and Concord, Massachusetts. Second Continental Congress opens in Philadelphia. George Washington becomes commander-in-chief of the Continental army.

1776—Declaration of Independence is adopted on July 4.

1777—Congress adopts the American flag with thirteen stars and thirteen stripes. John Adams is sent to France to negotiate peace treaty.

1778—France declares war against Great Britain and becomes U.S. ally.

1779—British surrender to Americans at Vincennes. Thomas Jefferson is elected governor of Virginia. James Madison is elected to the Continental Congress.

1780—Benedict Arnold, first American traitor, defects to the British.

1781—Articles of Confederation go into effect. Cornwallis surrenders to George Washington at Yorktown, ending the American Revolution.

1782—American commissioners, including John Adams, sign peace treaty with British in Paris. Thomas Jefferson's wife, Martha, dies. Martin Van Buren is born in Kinderhook, New York.

1784—Zachary Taylor is born near Barboursville, Virginia.

1785—Congress adopts the dollar as the unit of currency. John Adams is made minister to Great Britain. Thomas Jefferson is appointed minister to France.

1786—Shays's Rebellion begins in Massachusetts.

1787—Constitutional Convention assembles in Philadelphia, with George Washington presiding; U.S. Constitution is adopted. Delaware, New Jersey, and Pennsylvania become states.

1788—Virginia, South Carolina, New York, Connecticut, New Hampshire, Maryland, and Massachusetts become states. U.S. Constitution is ratified. New York City is declared U.S. capital.

1789—Presidential electors elect George Washington and John Adams as first president and vice-president. Thomas Jefferson is appointed secretary of state. North Carolina becomes a state. French Revolution begins.

1790—Supreme Court meets for the first time. Rhode Island becomes a state. First national census in the U.S. counts 3,929,214 persons. John Tyler is born in Charles City County, Virginia.

1791—Vermont enters the Union. U.S. Bill of Rights, the first ten amendments to the Constitution, goes into effect. District of Columbia is established. James Buchanan is born in Stony Batter, Pennsylvania.

1792—Thomas Paine publishes *The Rights of Man*. Kentucky becomes a state. Two political parties are formed in the U.S., Federalist and Republican. Washington is elected to a second term, with Adams as vice-president.

1793—War between France and Britain begins; U.S. declares neutrality. Eli Whitney invents the cotton gin; cotton production and slave labor increase in the South.

1794—Eleventh Amendment to the Constitution is passed, limiting federal courts' power. "Whiskey Rebellion" in Pennsylvania protests federal whiskey tax. James Madison marries Dolley Payne Todd.

1795—George Washington signs the Jay Treaty with Great Britain. Treaty of San Lorenzo, between U.S. and Spain, settles Florida boundary and gives U.S. right to navigate the Mississippi. James Polk is born near Pineville, North Carolina.

1796—Tennessee enters the Union. Washington gives his Farewell Address, refusing a third presidential term. John Adams is elected president and Thomas Jefferson vice-president.

1797—Adams recommends defense measures against possible war with France. Napoleon Bonaparte and his army march against Austrians in Italy. U.S. population is about 4,900,000.

1798—Washington is named commander-in-chief of the U.S. Army. Department of the Navy is created. Alien and Sedition Acts are passed. Napoleon's troops invade Egypt and Switzerland.

1799—George Washington dies at Mount Vernon, New York. James Monroe is elected governor of Virginia. French Revolution ends. Napoleon becomes ruler of France.

1800—Thomas Jefferson and Aaron Burr tie for president. U.S. capital is moved from Philadelphia to Washington, D.C. The White House is built as presidents' home. Spain returns Louisiana to France. Millard Fillmore is born in Locke, New York.

1801—After thirty-six ballots, House of Representatives elects Thomas Jefferson president, making Burr vice-president. James Madison is named secretary of state.

1802—Congress abolishes excise taxes. U.S. Military Academy is founded at West Point, New York.

1803—Ohio enters the Union. Louisiana Purchase treaty is signed with France, greatly expanding U.S. territory.

1804—Twelfth Amendment to the Constitution rules that president and vice-president be elected separately. Alexander Hamilton is killed by Vice-President Aaron Burr in a duel. Orleans Territory is established. Napoleon crowns himself emperor of France. Franklin Pierce is born in Hillsborough Lower Village, New Hampshire.

1805—Thomas Jefferson begins his second term as president. Lewis and Clark expedition reaches the Pacific Ocean.

1806—Coinage of silver dollars is stopped; resumes in 1836.

1807—Aaron Burr is acquitted in treason trial. Embargo Act closes U.S. ports to trade.

1808—James Madison is elected president. Congress outlaws importing slaves from Africa. Andrew Johnson is born in Raleigh, North Carolina.

1809—Abraham Lincoln is born near Hodgenville, Kentucky.

1810—U.S. population is 7,240,000.

1811—William Henry Harrison defeats Indians at Tippecanoe. Monroe is named secretary of state.

1812—Louisiana becomes a state. U.S. declares war on Britain (War of 1812). James Madison is reelected president. Napoleon invades Russia.

1813—British forces take Fort Niagara and Buffalo, New York.

1814—Francis Scott Key writes "The Star-Spangled Banner." British troops burn much of Washington, D.C., including the White House. Treaty of Ghent ends War of 1812. James Monroe becomes secretary of war.

1815—Napoleon meets his final defeat at Battle of Waterloo.

1816—James Monroe is elected president. Indiana becomes a state.

1817—Mississippi becomes a state. Construction on Erie Canal begins.

1818—Illinois enters the Union. The present thirteen-stripe flag is adopted. Border between U.S. and Canada is agreed upon.

1819—Alabama becomes a state. U.S. purchases Florida from Spain. Thomas Jefferson establishes the University of Virginia.

1820—James Monroe is reelected. In the Missouri Compromise, Maine enters the Union as a free (non-slave) state.

1821—Missouri enters the Union as a slave state. Santa Fe Trail opens the American Southwest. Mexico declares independence from Spain. Napoleon Bonaparte dies.

1822—U.S. recognizes Mexico and Colombia. Liberia in Africa is founded as a home for freed slaves. Ulysses S. Grant is born in Point Pleasant, Ohio. Rutherford B. Hayes is born in Delaware, Ohio.

1823—Monroe Doctrine closes North and South America to European colonizing or invasion.

1824—House of Representatives elects John Quincy Adams president when none of the four candidates wins a majority in national election. Mexico becomes a republic.

1825—Erie Canal is opened. U.S. population is 11,300,000.

1826—Thomas Jefferson and John Adams both die on July 4, the fiftieth anniversary of the Declaration of Independence.

1828—Andrew Jackson is elected president. Tariff of Abominations is passed, cutting imports.

1829—James Madison attends Virginia's constitutional convention. Slavery is abolished in Mexico. Chester A. Arthur is born in Fairfield, Vermont.

1830—Indian Removal Act to resettle Indians west of the Mississippi is approved.

1831—James Monroe dies in New York City. James A. Garfield is born in Orange, Ohio. Cyrus McCormick develops his reaper.

1832—Andrew Jackson, nominated by the new Democratic Party, is reelected president.

1833—Britain abolishes slavery in its colonies. Benjamin Harrison is born in North Bend, Ohio.

1835—Federal government becomes debt-free for the first time.

1836—Martin Van Buren becomes president. Texas wins independence from Mexico. Arkansas joins the Union. James Madison dies at Montpelier, Virginia.

1837—Michigan enters the Union. U.S. population is 15,900,000. Grover Cleveland is born in Caldwell, New Jersey.

1840—William Henry Harrison is elected president.

1841—President Harrison dies in Washington, D.C., one month after inauguration. Vice-President John Tyler succeeds him.

1843—William McKinley is born in Niles, Ohio.

1844—James Knox Polk is elected president. Samuel Morse sends first telegraphic message.

1845—Texas and Florida become states. Potato famine in Ireland causes massive emigration from Ireland to U.S. Andrew Jackson dies near Nashville, Tennessee.

1846—Iowa enters the Union. War with Mexico begins.

1847—U.S. captures Mexico City.

1848—John Quincy Adams dies in Washington, D.C. Zachary Taylor becomes president. Treaty of Guadalupe Hidalgo ends Mexico-U.S. war. Wisconsin becomes a state.

1849—James Polk dies in Nashville, Tennessee.

1850—President Taylor dies in Washington, D.C.; Vice-President Millard Fillmore succeeds him. California enters the Union, breaking tie between slave and free states.

1852—Franklin Pierce is elected president.

1853—Gadsden Purchase transfers Mexican territory to U.S.

1854—"War for Bleeding Kansas" is fought between slave and free states.

1855—Czar Nicholas I of Russia dies, succeeded by Alexander II.

1856—James Buchanan is elected president. In Massacre of Potawatomi Creek, Kansas-slavers are murdered by free-staters. Woodrow Wilson is born in Staunton, Virginia.

1857—William Howard Taft is born in Cincinnati, Ohio.

1858—Minnesota enters the Union. Theodore Roosevelt is born in New York City.

1859—Oregon becomes a state.

1860—Abraham Lincoln is elected president; South Carolina secedes from the Union in protest.

1861—Arkansas, Tennessee, North Carolina, and Virginia secede. Kansas enters the Union as a free state. Civil War begins.

1862—Union forces capture Fort Henry, Roanoke Island, Fort Donelson, Jacksonville, and New Orleans; Union armies are defeated at the battles of Bull Run and Fredericksburg. Martin Van Buren dies in Kinderhook, New York. John Tyler dies near Charles City, Virginia.

1863—Lincoln issues Emancipation Proclamation: all slaves held in rebelling territories are declared free. West Virginia becomes a state.

1864—Abraham Lincoln is reelected. Nevada becomes a state.

1865—Lincoln is assassinated in Washington, D.C., and succeeded by Andrew Johnson. U.S. Civil War ends on May 26. Thirteenth Amendment abolishes slavery. Warren G. Harding is born in Blooming Grove, Ohio.

1867—Nebraska becomes a state. U.S. buys Alaska from Russia for $7,200,000. Reconstruction Acts are passed.

1868—President Johnson is impeached for violating Tenure of Office Act, but is acquitted by Senate. Ulysses S. Grant is elected president. Fourteenth Amendment prohibits voting discrimination. James Buchanan dies in Lancaster, Pennsylvania.

1869—Franklin Pierce dies in Concord, New Hampshire.

1870—Fifteenth Amendment gives blacks the right to vote.

1872—Grant is reelected over Horace Greeley. General Amnesty Act pardons ex-Confederates. Calvin Coolidge is born in Plymouth Notch, Vermont.

1874—Millard Fillmore dies in Buffalo, New York. Herbert Hoover is born in West Branch, Iowa.

1875—Andrew Johnson dies in Carter's Station, Tennessee.

1876—Colorado enters the Union. "Custer's last stand": he and his men are massacred by Sioux Indians at Little Big Horn, Montana.

1877—Rutherford B. Hayes is elected president as all disputed votes are awarded to him.

1880—James A. Garfield is elected president.

1881—President Garfield is assassinated and dies in Elberon, New Jersey. Vice-President Chester A. Arthur succeeds him.

1882—U.S. bans Chinese immigration. Franklin D. Roosevelt is born in Hyde Park, New York.

1884—Grover Cleveland is elected president. Harry S. Truman is born in Lamar, Missouri.

1885—Ulysses S. Grant dies in Mount McGregor, New York.

1886—Statue of Liberty is dedicated. Chester A. Arthur dies in New York City.

1888—Benjamin Harrison is elected president.

1889—North Dakota, South Dakota, Washington, and Montana become states.

1890—Dwight D. Eisenhower is born in Denison, Texas. Idaho and Wyoming become states.

1892—Grover Cleveland is elected president.

1893—Rutherford B. Hayes dies in Fremont, Ohio.

1896—William McKinley is elected president. Utah becomes a state.

1898—U.S. declares war on Spain over Cuba.

1900—McKinley is reelected. Boxer Rebellion against foreigners in China begins.

1901—McKinley is assassinated by anarchist Leon Czolgosz in Buffalo, New York; Theodore Roosevelt becomes president. Benjamin Harrison dies in Indianapolis, Indiana.

1902—U.S. acquires perpetual control over Panama Canal.

1903—Alaskan frontier is settled.

1904—Russian-Japanese War breaks out. Theodore Roosevelt wins presidential election.

1905—Treaty of Portsmouth signed, ending Russian-Japanese War.

1906—U.S. troops occupy Cuba.

1907—President Roosevelt bars all Japanese immigration. Oklahoma enters the Union.

1908—William Howard Taft becomes president. Grover Cleveland dies in Princeton, New Jersey. Lyndon B. Johnson is born near Stonewall, Texas.

1909—NAACP is founded under W.E.B. DuBois

1910—China abolishes slavery.

1911—Chinese Revolution begins. Ronald Reagan is born in Tampico, Illinois.

1912—Woodrow Wilson is elected president. Arizona and New Mexico become states.

1913—Federal income tax is introduced in U.S. through the Sixteenth Amendment. Richard Nixon is born in Yorba Linda, California. Gerald Ford is born in Omaha, Nebraska.

1914—World War I begins.

1915—British liner *Lusitania* is sunk by German submarine.

1916—Wilson is reelected president.

1917—U.S. breaks diplomatic relations with Germany. Czar Nicholas of Russia abdicates as revolution begins. U.S. declares war on Austria-Hungary. John F. Kennedy is born in Brookline, Massachusetts.

1918—Wilson proclaims "Fourteen Points" as war aims. On November 11, armistice is signed between Allies and Germany.

1919—Eighteenth Amendment prohibits sale and manufacture of intoxicating liquors. Wilson presides over first League of Nations; wins Nobel Peace Prize. Theodore Roosevelt dies in Oyster Bay, New York.

1920—Nineteenth Amendment (women's suffrage) is passed. Warren Harding is elected president.

1921—Adolf Hitler's stormtroopers begin to terrorize political opponents.

1922—Irish Free State is established. Soviet states form USSR. Benito Mussolini forms Fascist government in Italy.

1923—President Harding dies in San Francisco, California; he is succeeded by Vice-President Calvin Coolidge.

1924—Coolidge is elected president. Woodrow Wilson dies in Washington, D.C. James Carter is born in Plains, Georgia. George Bush is born in Milton, Massachusetts.

1925—Hitler reorganizes Nazi Party and publishes first volume of *Mein Kampf.*

1926—Fascist youth organizations founded in Germany and Italy. Republic of Lebanon proclaimed.

1927—Stalin becomes Soviet dictator. Economic conference in Geneva attended by fifty-two nations.

1928—Herbert Hoover is elected president. U.S. and many other nations sign Kellogg-Briand pacts to outlaw war.

1929—Stock prices in New York crash on "Black Thursday"; the Great Depression begins.

1930—Bank of U.S. and its many branches close (most significant bank failure of the year). William Howard Taft dies in Washington, D.C.

1931—Emigration from U.S. exceeds immigration for first time as Depression deepens.

1932—Franklin D. Roosevelt wins presidential election in a Democratic landslide.

1933—First concentration camps are erected in Germany. U.S. recognizes USSR and resumes trade. Twenty-First Amendment repeals prohibition. Calvin Coolidge dies in Northampton, Massachusetts.

1934—Severe dust storms hit Plains states. President Roosevelt passes U.S. Social Security Act.

1936—Roosevelt is reelected. Spanish Civil War begins. Hitler and Mussolini form Rome-Berlin Axis.

1937—Roosevelt signs Neutrality Act.

1938—Roosevelt sends appeal to Hitler and Mussolini to settle European problems amicably.

1939—Germany takes over Czechoslovakia and invades Poland, starting World War II.

1940—Roosevelt is reelected for a third term.

1941—Japan bombs Pearl Harbor, U.S. declares war on Japan. Germany and Italy declare war on U.S.; U.S. then declares war on them.

1942—Allies agree not to make separate peace treaties with the enemies. U.S. government transfers more than 100,000 Nisei (Japanese-Americans) from west coast to inland concentration camps.

1943—Allied bombings of Germany begin.

1944—Roosevelt is reelected for a fourth term. Allied forces invade Normandy on D-Day.

1945—President Franklin D. Roosevelt dies in Warm Springs, Georgia; Vice-President Harry S. Truman succeeds him. Mussolini is killed; Hitler commits suicide. Germany surrenders. U.S. drops atomic bomb on Hiroshima; Japan surrenders: end of World War II.

1946—U.N. General Assembly holds its first session in London. Peace conference of twenty-one nations is held in Paris.

1947—Peace treaties are signed in Paris. "Cold War" is in full swing.

1948—U.S. passes Marshall Plan Act, providing $17 billion in aid for Europe. U.S. recognizes new nation of Israel. India and Pakistan become free of British rule. Truman is elected president.

1949—Republic of Eire is proclaimed in Dublin. Russia blocks land route access from Western Germany to Berlin; airlift begins. U.S., France, and Britain agree to merge their zones of occupation in West Germany. Apartheid program begins in South Africa.

1950—Riots in Johannesburg, South Africa, against apartheid. North Korea invades South Korea. U.N. forces land in South Korea and recapture Seoul.

1951—Twenty-Second Amendment limits president to two terms.

1952—Dwight D. Eisenhower resigns as supreme commander in Europe and is elected president.

1953—Stalin dies; struggle for power in Russia follows. Rosenbergs are executed for espionage.

1954—U.S. and Japan sign mutual defense agreement.

1955—Blacks in Montgomery, Alabama, boycott segregated bus lines.

1956—Eisenhower is reelected president. Soviet troops march into Hungary.

1957—U.S. agrees to withdraw ground forces from Japan. Russia launches first satellite, *Sputnik*.

1958—European Common Market comes into being. Fidel Castro begins war against Batista government in Cuba.

1959—Alaska becomes the forty-ninth state. Hawaii becomes fiftieth state. Castro becomes premier of Cuba. De Gaulle is proclaimed president of the Fifth Republic of France.

1960—Historic debates between Senator John F. Kennedy and Vice-President Richard Nixon are televised. Kennedy is elected president. Brezhnev becomes president of USSR.

1961—Berlin Wall is constructed. Kennedy and Khrushchev confer in Vienna. In Bay of Pigs incident, Cubans trained by CIA attempt to overthrow Castro.

1962—U.S. military council is established in South Vietnam.

1963—Riots and beatings by police and whites mark civil rights demonstrations in Birmingham, Alabama; 30,000 troops are called out, Martin Luther King, Jr., is arrested. Freedom marchers descend on Washington, D.C., to demonstrate. President Kennedy is assassinated in Dallas, Texas; Vice-President Lyndon B. Johnson is sworn in as president.

1964—U.S. aircraft bomb North Vietnam. Johnson is elected president. Herbert Hoover dies in New York City.

1965—U.S. combat troops arrive in South Vietnam.

1966—Thousands protest U.S. policy in Vietnam. National Guard quells race riots in Chicago.

1967—Six-Day War between Israel and Arab nations.

1968—Martin Luther King, Jr., is assassinated in Memphis, Tennessee. Senator Robert Kennedy is assassinated in Los Angeles. Riots and police brutality take place at Democratic National Convention in Chicago. Richard Nixon is elected president. Czechoslovakia is invaded by Soviet troops.

1969—Dwight D. Eisenhower dies in Washington, D.C. Hundreds of thousands of people in several U.S. cities demonstrate against Vietnam War.

1970—Four Vietnam War protesters are killed by National Guardsmen at Kent State University in Ohio.

1971—Twenty-Sixth Amendment allows eighteen-year-olds to vote.

1972—Nixon visits Communist China; is reelected president in near-record landslide. Watergate affair begins when five men are arrested in the Watergate hotel complex in Washington, D.C. Nixon announces resignations of aides Haldeman, Ehrlichman, and Dean and Attorney General Kleindienst as a result of Watergate-related charges. Harry S. Truman dies in Kansas City, Missouri.

1973—Vice-President Spiro Agnew resigns; Gerald Ford is named vice-president. Vietnam peace treaty is formally approved after nineteen months of negotiations. Lyndon B. Johnson dies in San Antonio, Texas.

1974—As a result of Watergate cover-up, impeachment is considered; Nixon resigns and Ford becomes president. Ford pardons Nixon and grants limited amnesty to Vietnam War draft evaders and military deserters.

1975—U.S. civilians are evacuated from Saigon, South Vietnam, as Communist forces complete takeover of South Vietnam.

1976—U.S. celebrates its Bicentennial. James Earl Carter becomes president.

1977—Carter pardons most Vietnam draft evaders, numbering some 10,000.

1980—Ronald Reagan is elected president.

1981—President Reagan is shot in the chest in assassination attempt. Sandra Day O'Connor is appointed first woman justice of the Supreme Court.

1983—U.S. troops invade island of Grenada.

1984—Reagan is reelected president. Democratic candidate Walter Mondale's running mate, Geraldine Ferraro, is the first woman selected for vice-president by a major U.S. political party.

1985—Soviet Communist Party secretary Konstantin Chernenko dies; Mikhail Gorbachev succeeds him. U.S. and Soviet officials discuss arms control in Geneva. Reagan and Gorbachev hold summit conference in Geneva. Racial tensions accelerate in South Africa.

1986—Space shuttle *Challenger* explodes shortly after takeoff; crew of seven dies. U.S. bombs bases in Libya. Corazon Aquino defeats Ferdinand Marcos in Philippine presidential election.

1987—Iraqi missile rips the U.S. frigate *Stark* in the Persian Gulf, killing thirty-seven American sailors. Congress holds hearings to investigate sale of U.S. arms to Iran to finance Nicaraguan *contra* movement.

1988—President Reagan and Soviet leader Gorbachev sign INF treaty, eliminating intermediate nuclear forces. Severe drought sweeps the United States. George Bush is elected president.

1989—East Germany opens Berlin Wall, allowing citizens free exit. Communists lose control of governments in Poland, Romania, and Czechoslovakia. Chinese troops massacre over 1,000 pro-democracy student demonstrators in Beijing's Tiananmen Square.

1990—Iraq annexes Kuwait, provoking the threat of war. East and West Germany are reunited. The Cold War between the United States and the Soviet Union comes to a close. Several Soviet republics make moves toward independence.

1991—Backed by a coalition of members of the United Nations, U.S. troops drive Iraqis from Kuwait. Latvia, Lithuania, and Estonia withdraw from the USSR. The Soviet Union dissolves as its republics secede to form a Commonwealth of Independent States.

1992—U.N. forces fail to stop fighting in territories of former Yugoslavia. More than fifty people are killed and more than six hundred buildings burned in rioting in Los Angeles. U.S. unemployment reaches eight-year high. Hurricane Andrew devastates southern Florida and parts of Louisiana. International relief supplies and troops are sent to combat famine and violence in Somalia.

1993—U.S.-led forces use airplanes and missiles to attack military targets in Iraq. William Jefferson Clinton becomes the forty-second U.S. president.

1994—Richard M. Nixon dies in New York City.

Index

Page numbers in boldface type indicate illustrations.

abolitionists, 7-8
Adams, Abigail (sister), 16
Adams, Abigail Smith (mother), 11-12, **12**, 18
Adams, Charles (son), 33, 47
Adams, George (son), 48
Adams, John (father), 9, 11-12, **12**, 14, 25-26, 29, 71, **71**
Adams, John (son), 48
Adams, Louisa Catherine Johnson (wife), 24-25, **25**, 27-28, 34
Adams, Thomas (brother), 23
Alexander I, 34-35, **36**
Alfred (ship), 23
American Civil War, 47, 55
American Revolution, 9, 11, 13, 17, 89
American Southwest, 86
Atlantic Ocean, 23, 33, 49
Baltic Sea, 36
Battle of New Orleans, 47
Battle of Waterloo, 47
Bayard, James, **42**
bedroom of Adams, **10**
Belgium, **40**, 41
Benton, Thomas Hart, 88
Berlin, 26
birthplace of Adams, **10**, 11
birthplace of John Adams, **10**
Bolívar, Simón, 58, **58**
Bonaparte, Napoleon, 37, **37**, 38-39, **39**, 47
borders of U.S., 53-54
Boston (ship), 14
Boston Common, **20**
Braintree, Massachusetts, 11
British aggressions, **13**, 29-30, **30**, 37, 39, **46**
Bunker Hill, 13, **13**
Bunker Hill Monument, **72**
burial of Adams, 89
Calhoun, John C., 62
campaign poster, **76**
Canning, Stratford, 56
Capitol building, **29**
Cherokee Indians, 73
Chesapeake (ship), **30**
Clay, Henry, 41-42, **42**, 43, 61-62, 63-64, 68-69, 81, 87
Clinton, DeWitt, **74**
Congress, 68, 80, 83, **84**, 86
Continental Congress, 14
Crawford, William, 63-64
customs, Russian, 36

death of John Adams, 70
death of John Quincy Adams, 86-88, **87**, **88**
Declaration of Independence, 71
Democratic-Republican party, 77
Dickens, Charles, 84
diplomatic services of Adams, 23-26, 33-39, 41-43, 47-49
duel (involving Adams), 69
education of Adams, 12, 14-16, 18-19
"Era of Good Feeling," 51, 57
Erie Canal, 73, **74-75**
Embargo Act of 1807, 30-31
Faneuil Hall (Boston), 89
Federalist Party, 26-27, 29, 31
Fisher, Davis, 87
Florida, 51-53, 72
formal entertaining, **60**, **67**
Fourth of July, 70, **70**
France, 14, 18, 29
Franklin, Benjamin, 17
Frederick William, king of Prussia, 26
freedom of speech, 86
French army, 24, 37, **37**
"gag rule," 8-9, 83-84, 86
Gallatin, Albert, **42**
Gambier, Lord, **43**
Ghent, **40**, 41
Greco, Count, 16
Hague, The, 17, **22**, 24
Hampshire Gazette, 30
Harvard College, 18-19, **19**
"Hero of New Orleans," 62, 78
hobbies of Adams, 33
Holland, 17, 21, 24
Holmes, Issac, 88
homes of John Adams, **10**, **27**
homes of John Quincy Adams, **5**, **10**, 11, 79, **80**
House of Representatives, 7-9, 63-64, 80, 84, 86
Hughes, Christopher, 59
inaugural ball, 65
Independence Day celebrations, 70, **70**
Indian peace medal, **4**
industrialization, 57, 73
Jackson, Andrew, **46**, 47, 52, **60**, 62, 76, 77-79
Jackson, Rachel, 78
Jay, John, 17, 23
Jefferson, Thomas, 26, 28, 30, 70-71, **71**
Johnson, Andrew, 8
Johnson, Joshua, 24

Lafayette, Marquis de, 72, **72**, 73
law career of Adams, 19-20
Leiden (Dutch city), 15, **15**
Leopard (ship), 30
Lloyd, James, Jr., 31
Louisiana Territory, 28-29
Lyman, Theodore, 29
Madison, James, 33, 39
map of United States, **53**
Marshall, John, 65, **65**
Meridian Hill, 79
Mexico, 86
Michigan Territory, 73
Missouri Compromise, 55
Missouri Territory, 54
Monroe Doctrine, 58-59
Monroe, James, 49, **49**, **50**, 51-52, 57-59,
    59, 64-65
Monticello, 71
monument to the Adamses, **89**
Moose Island, 43
Moscow, 37-38, **38**, **39**
naval academy, 68
Neva River (Russia), 35, **35**
New Orleans, 47
Niemen River (Russia), 37
New York Times, 7
"Old Hickory," 78
"Old Man Eloquent," 9, 86, 89
Pacific Ocean, 53
Paine, Thomas, 20
Passy Academy, 14
peace negotiations, 39, 41-43, **43**
personality traits of Adams, 18-19, 41, 62, 84
Peter the Great, statue of, **16**
political cartoons, **40**, **62**, **78**
political parties, 26-27, 29, 31
portraits and pictures of Adams, **2**, **6**, **25**,
    48, **50**, **60**, **81**, **82**, **84**, **87**, **88**
Portugal, 25
Potomac River, 69
presidency of Adams, 61-75, 77

presidential electors, 63
presidential mansion, 66, **66**
Prussia, 26, 38
pseudonyms of Adams, 20-21
"Publicola," 20
Quincy, Massachusetts, 11
Randolph, Edmund, 24
Randolph, John, 69, **69**
retirement of Adams, 7, 79
Rights of Man, The, 20, **21**
Rochester, New York, 9
Royall, Anne, 68
Russia, 15-16, **16**, **32**, 33-35, **35**, 36-38,
    36, **38**, 39, **39**
Saint Isaac's Cathedral, **35**
Saint James Palace, 48
Saint Petersburg, 15-16, 16, **32**, 33-35,
    35, 37, 39
Salem Gazette, 31
San Martín, Jośe de, 58, **58**
secretary of state, Quincy's term as, 51-59
Seminole Indians, 51-52, **52**
Seminole War, 52, **52**
slavery, 7-9, 54-55, **55**, 83-85, **85**
South America, 58
Spain, 51-53, 56, 58
stroke, suffered by Adams, 86, **87**
Supreme Court, **65**
Talmadge, James, 54
Texas, 86
Thomas, Jesse, 54
trade embargo, 30-31
Treaty of Ghent, 40, 43, **43**, **46**
Treaty of Paris, 17, **17**
Van Rensselaer, Stephen, 64
wardrobe of Adams, 18, 61
War of 1812, 37-39, **40**, 41-43, **44-46**
Washington, D.C., 28, **28-29**, 34, 83
Washington, George, 14, 20-21, 25-26
White House, 66, **66**
wilderness (American), **57**
Winnebago Indians, 73

About the Author

Zachary Kent grew up in Little Falls, New Jersey, and received an English degree from St. Lawrence University. Following college he worked at a New York City literary agency for two years and then launched his writing career. To support himself while writing, he has worked as a taxi driver, a shipping clerk, and a house painter. Mr. Kent has had a lifelong interest in American history. Studying the U.S. presidents was his childhood hobby. His collection of presidential items includes books, pictures, and games, as well as several autographed letters.